Praise for
How

"I've spent over 25 years help... ...ir possessions - including cleaning som... ...est homes in America - and many people I meet say, 'I wish I met you 2 years ago.' With *How to Move Your Parents (and still be on speaking terms)*, you'll have the expert guidance you need, in the palm of your hand, exactly when you need it.

Marty Stevens-Heebner has taken all the chaos, stress, and unexpected hurdles of moving an older loved one and wrapped them into a guide that's as practical as it is reassuring.

Marty doesn't just give you a to-do list (though the checklists are fantastic). She walks you through the even more important emotional side of things, too—how to manage family dynamics, make tough decisions, and avoid the common pitfalls that turn a move into a meltdown. And she does it all with warmth, humor, and a deep understanding of what families actually go through.

Marty has been a leader in the moving and downsizing world for over a decade, and her expertise and poise will help you and your family turn this challenging time into an amazing journey."

Matt Paxton, *Filthy Fortunes, Legacy List with Matt Paxton, HOARDERS*

"If you're facing the daunting task of moving your aging parents—decades of belongings, complex emotions, and a pressing timeline—*How to Move Your Parents (and still be on speaking terms)* is the essential lifeline you need. Drawing on years of professional expertise, Marty Stevens-Heebner delivers a compassionate, practical, and comprehensive guide to managing this significant life transition with confidence and grace.

Packed with strategic insights, detailed checklists, and candid advice on navigating intricate family dynamics, this book transforms an overwhelming challenge into a step-by-step, manageable process. With Marty's expert guidance, you'll not only streamline the moving experience but also preserve the relationships that matter most. Read it, apply its wisdom, and breathe easier—Marty is your trusted companion every step of the way."

Mary Kay Buysse - Co-Executive Director, National Association of Senior & Specialty Move Managers

"What an amazing resource this is! I wish I had it when I needed to clean out my mother's apartment after moving her to my house - and when my family moved from our house of 30 years to a new home. All of this information in one place is incredible! So many tips inside each chapter and checklists to help you every step of the process.

Helping your parents move or downsize can often feel daunting, leaving you overwhelmed and unsure where to begin. Thankfully, Marty-Stevens Heebner's insightful book, *How to Move Your Parents (and still be on speaking terms)*, is here to transform that anxiety into empowerment.

In each chapter, you'll find practical advice, helpful Moving Moments, Inside Scoop, Smart Move Tips, and meticulously crafted worksheets. With compassion and expertise, Marty shares this valuable information, while also recognizing the emotional journey that often comes with the challenges of a physical move.

If you're facing the challenge of helping your parents with a move and wondering, "How am I ever going to manage this?!" let *How to Move Your Parents (and still be on speaking terms)* be your trusted companion on this journey. It's the guidance you need to navigate this experience without losing your mind!"

Rosanne Corcoran - Podcast Host, *Daughterhood*

"Moving is stressful, but when you add an aging parent to the mix, you have a recipe for strain, fights, and possibly failure. Thankfully, families have Marty Stevens-Heebner. She has expertly put a decade of experience to paper for everyone's benefit.

From sorting through decades of belongings to handling estate sales and move-day logistics, Marty's expertise shines through. She understands the real challenges families face and delivers solutions that truly work. All of this experience is combined with thoughtful and useful checklists that will keep everyone on schedule—and quite possibly, still on speaking terms by the end.

If you are moving or guiding a loved one through the relocation process, do yourself a favor and get this book!"

Todd Emrick - Director of Business Development, Wheaton-Bekins Worldwide Moving

"With her signature efficiency, humor and compassion, Marty Stevens-Heebner lays out a comprehensive, structured roadmap on how to plan and execute a later-life move. Short chapters, frequent subheads and a detailed Table of Contents make *How to Move Your Parents (and still be on speaking terms)* especially easy to use. Packed with wisdom, common sense and practicality, this is a must-have book for anyone planning a complex, emotional move --- in short, for everyone."

Margit Novack, the founder of NASMM, now retired, and author of *Squint: Re-Visioning the Second Half of Life*

HOW TO MOVE YOUR PARENTS

(and still be on speaking terms)

MARTY STEVENS-HEEBNER

Copyright © 2025 by Marty Stevens-Heebner

All rights reserved. No part of this book may be reproduced in any form or by any electronic or mechanical means, including information storage and retrieval systems, without written permission from the publisher, except by a reviewer who may quote brief passages in a review. For information, please visit www.MartyStevensHeebner.com.

This publication is designed to provide accurate and authoritative information in regard to the subject matter covered. It is sold with the understanding that neither the author nor the publisher is engaged in rendering legal, investment, accounting or other professional services. While the publisher and author have used their best efforts in preparing this book, they make no representations or warranties with respect to the accuracy or completeness of the contents of this book and specifically disclaim any implied warranties of merchantability or fitness for a particular purpose. No warranty may be created or extended by sales representatives or written sales materials. The advice and strategies contained herein may not be suitable for your situation. You should consult with a professional when appropriate. Neither the publisher nor the author shall be liable for any loss of profit or any other commercial damages, including but not limited to special, incidental, consequential, personal, or other damages.

Cover Design: Plethora Creative & Marty Stevens-Heebner

Interior Text Design: Plethora Creative

This book is dedicated to the generous planet we live on, the night sky with its inspiring stars and luminous moon, and (quoting from Maureen Stapleton's 1981 Academy Awards' acceptance speech) "everybody I ever met in my entire life"…

… for you have taught me everything I know.

Contents

How to Move Your Parents (and still be on speaking terms) includes all the checklists you'll need as you journey through the moving process. **These checklists are also available online** to make things easier. Please check the "Resources" page toward the end of this book to find the link and additional resources.

Introduction	13
Guide Structure	14
How to Get the Most Out of This Guide	15
ACT ONE	**17**
Awareness and the Arc of Moving	**19**
Shaking Hands with Your Emotions	21
Move Management Checklist	*25*
Create a Plan	**35**
It'll Save Time, Money, and Sanity	35
Floor Planning Checklist	*43*
Change of Address List	*50*
Who Can (and Really Will) Help You for Free	**66**
Hiring Help & How to Do It	**69**
Professionals & Services to Consider	*78*
Mental Maintenance: How to Keep Your Head from Exploding	**83**
Tackling the Acreage of Memories	**85**
Sorting & Downsizing Action Plan	*89*
Safety is Everyone's Responsibility	**97**
11 Vital Safety Rules	97
Safety Checklist	*104*
ACT TWO	***107***
Time to Dig In – But Where?	**109**

Top Preparation Tips for Sorting and Downsizing	109
The C.L.E.A.N.S.E. Concept	**112**
Straightforward Methods to Simplify, Sort, & Downsize	112
Here's a Quick C.L.E.A.N.S.E. Primer	112
The Obstacle of Memory	**134**
The Clothing Quagmire	135
Culling Crowded Closets	137
Undiscovered Treasures in Unexpected Places	**144**
Photographs	**150**
Your Family's History, Illustrated.	150
The "ABC" Method of sorting photos	152
How to Name Digital Photo Files	*157*
Photo Sorting Supplies	*160*
Vital Documents & How to Find Them	**162**
Vital Documents & Keys	*166*
How to Pack & Label Like a Pro	**172**
The Basic Rules of Packing	175
Fragile Items	177
Electronic Items	178
Kitchen Items	179
Bookcases	180
Books and Vinyl Records	180
Clothing: So Hard to Sort, but so Easy to Pack	181
Linens and Towels	182
Weapons, Ammunition, Explosives, Oxygen Tanks & Other Combustibles – Including Oxygen Tanks	182

Local Moves vs. Long-Distance Moves	183
How to Label your Moving Boxes	184
Timeline for Packing	186
Packing Supplies Checklist	*190*
Packing List	*191*
Beware the Days Just Before Move Day	**196**
ACT THREE	***201***
Move Day (i.e., Holy CRAP Day)	**203**
Local Moves - Part 1: Moving Out	205
Local Moves - Part 2: Moving In	207
Longer Distance Moves: Keeping Track of the Truck	209
Move Day Checklist	*211*
Unpacking…and The Day After	**216**
The Basic Rules of Unpacking	218
Selling Your Possessions: Tame Those Expectations	**222**
Estate Sales & Auction Companies	225
Garage Sale Preparation	*234*
Donations = Giving Gifts to Strangers in Need	**241**
Clear Out Checklist	*248*
Before You Take a Bow	**254**
Afterword: The Emptied Home	**256**
Resources	257
Acknowledgements	259
About the Author	261

Introduction

As someone bridging the Baby Boomer and Gen X populations, I've been witness to, and part of, the tectonic shift upward in humanity's life expectancy. We're living substantially longer and healthier lives than we did 100 years ago. Some call this era the Age of Longevity.

Nevertheless, one thing remains as it has always been: eventually, older parents need to rely on their adult children for support, especially when remaining in their home becomes too onerous and, often, unsafe. This means they'll need to move to a new living situation, and that huge transition brings on challenges that even Hercules would struggle with.

This enormous undertaking frequently falls into one sibling's lap, usually a daughter's (ahem). If it's landed in *your* lap, then I wrote this book for you.

I've gathered all the know-how from my 12 years of senior move management experience into these pages. Since every client and situation has been unique, if it can happen during a move, my staff and I have seen it and solved it.

In these pages you'll find:

- Answers to questions I'm most often asked – and questions no one asks but *should* – to reveal the complete view of moving's rocky landscape.

- Thorough checklists and worksheets that cover the various stages of moving.
- A helpful hoard of tried-and-true techniques.

Think of this book as stress repellent. There's a lot to do, but you'll learn how to accomplish each step smoothly with clear explanations and how-to's for each task.

This guide also demystifies the emotional load of moving your parent(s), which can be the weightiest and most tangled part of the move, so you'll reduce strife within your family - and ease those cranky kinks in your neck and shoulders.

Guide Structure

I've structured this book as three acts, like a play or a movie, for two reasons. First, moving has a distinct beginning, middle, and end. Second, this will become a significant chapter of your family's story, with its own plot swerves, cast of characters, and meaning.

Act One: I'll lead you through the different tasks involved with your moving project, so you can create your own plan for a successful move.

Act Two: As in a film or stage play, this is usually the longest act. In moving, this second act includes sorting, downsizing, packing, and the other steps you'll do up until the evening before your move.

Act Three: This starts with the morning of Move Day. As in any television episode, the big action happens here, toward the end, but you'll discover how to pacify any mayhem.

People think that Move Day will be the worst of it. But it's followed by the day *after* Move Day, the morning when you all wake up to face stacks of unpacked boxes. After that, I'll show you how to disperse that ragged mountain of items left behind at the former home.

As you work through this huge shift, I'll be your ally from start to finish. It may seem like a dark, befuddling tunnel – but I've got the torch to guide you through to the end, each step of the way.

In other words, I've got your back!

How to Get the Most Out of This Guide

If possible, read this entire book before beginning your move preparation. That way, you'll be able to see the full landscape before you start this adventure. Understanding the whole process before you start will maximize the impact of the trusted process my colleagues and I have counted on for years.

More things to know as you read:

- To illustrate certain points, I tell stories about clients and colleagues but have changed everyone's name for all the usual reasons. Each of these experiences taught me something unique and extraordinary, and I hope they do the same for you.

- These are guidelines, not stone-carved commandments. Nothing is absolute. Every move presents its own unique narrative. Amend things where you need to.

- To maintain consistency, the scenario I've chosen focuses on an adult child in charge of their parents' move from a medium-sized home with a garage and attic.

- Where I write "parent," you can substitute "relative" or "friend," as many nieces, nephews, cousins, and friends have impressed me with their kindness and generous caregiving.

- If you're reading this book as the older parent (or relative), please know that some of the piques I address for adult children may well become your own annoyances. You may even want to consider giving your kids a copy of this guide.

Moving a parent may feel like climbing Everest. You will, at times, feel overwhelmed by exhaustion and confusion during this trek together. I refer to this as the "emotional flu" of moving and, just like any cold or flu bug, *you will get to the other side of it*.

Think of me as your veteran sherpa who'll get you up to the mountain's peak and safely back down again.

I'll be cheering you on, every step of the way.

Act One

Awareness and the Arc of Moving

World-changing fact: By the mid 2030s, more adults in the U.S. will be caring for their aging relatives than caring for children. That's a first in human history.

Our human population is growing older. Consider what's happening in the United States:

- 10,000 Baby Boomers turn 65 every single day.[1]

- Our population is older than it has ever been.[2] (No surprise, given that first statistic.)

- Over 50% of adults in their 40s – the "Sandwich Generation" - have at least one parent over the age of 65, and either a child younger than 18 or an adult child they support financially.[3]

As it is, for those feeling sandwiched, every day is an ungainly juggling act.

Then, one day, a throat-throttling pit lands in the mix: Your aging parents need to move from the home they've lived in for decades.

I launched my move management company, Clear Home Solutions, in 2013 to manage that huge pit so our clients wouldn't have to. We specialize in managing the moves of older adults with compassion and know-how, often incorporating other services such as home inventories, estate sales, and professional organizing as part of their project.

Yet our actual purpose is much more complex than simply getting our client's "stuff" from here to there. The focus of our business is *people*, not boxes and purging, as we help them sift through a lifetime's worth of treasured memories. A client we moved out of the country put it succinctly and splendidly: "What you really provide is peace of mind."

Moving is one of the biggest stressors in anyone's life, especially when it's from their home of 15, 25, or 40 years. The stress level is right up there with death, divorce, and losing a job - and there's research to prove it.[4]

It's not "relocation" so much as "dislocation," because anyone who moves feels out of joint until they've lived in their new home for at least a month. They'll need that time to get to know their new neighbors and neighborhood – and, for the record, a senior living community is most definitely a neighborhood filled with new neighbors to befriend.

A later-life move ripples through everyone and everything it touches, because it marks one of the greatest shifts in the life of an entire family. This kind of transition impacts all generations. I've held weeping grandchildren in my arms, together with their parents.

Understanding how to sooth stressful and anxious feelings will give you a framework to rest your weary head on. Becoming upset with yourself for having these emotions will only compound and enlarge the maelstrom inside you. Knowledge is not only power, but comfort as well.

Shaking Hands with Your Emotions

Take a moment to recall the last time you moved. Was it two years ago? Ten years? Forty years? Remember how daunting it was? And that it took a lot of time and struggle to complete that move and settle in? It probably took a while to feel truly at home in your new neighborhood.

Now imagine it from your older parents' point of view. Added to this moving mix are all of aging's challenges, which may include diminished mobility, loss of mental acuity, and the disorientation of leaving behind their comfortable and familiar paths of living for a new and unknown environment.

It's nerve-racking to experience, no matter which generation you are.

During many initial consultations, someone has said to me, "I'm losing it," "My brain is about to explode!," or "I don't know what's wrong with me." Something along those lines, usually with a curse word or two for emphasis.

If you, too, are feeling this way, it's called "moving," and it's *normal*. I realize that may be little comfort given that you're miserable, but just know it happens to everyone, especially when moving a parent.

Normal can mean:

- Forgetting your own name as well as everyone else's.
- Leaving your house keys next to the frozen peas in your freezer.
- Experiencing your car sputter beneath you as you run out of gas on the freeway because you forgot to fill the gas tank.

On those rare occasions when I've encountered a client who claims they feel fine, that they have it all under control, I pay attention - and I worry. They *think* they've manacled their anxiety but, at some point, it will gush out like a tidal wave.

To feel more comfortable with these feelings, think of them as the "emotional flu" of moving. Like the flu, a move does eventually come to an end. But, in the meantime, not feeling normal *is* normal. You'll most likely feel turbulence in your stomach, suffer through a headache or two, and you may even get the actual flu or a cold.[5]

Fortunately, the following set of remedies can ease these feelings and keep you as comfortable and functional as possible:

The Basics

- Get plenty of sleep.
- Make sure you drink plenty of water and drinks that are good for you, such as tea or fresh-squeezed juices.
- Keep your alcohol intake to a minimum or avoid it completely. Dehydration is an enemy and booze will dry you out.

- Eat well as frequently as you can.
- Exercise when you're able to.
  - I refer to some very active days as NGR days - No Gym Required – because you're on your feet for hours.

Taming Doubt and Thoughts of "I Should Be Doing More"

- Write down all your ideas and anything uncomfortable you may be feeling. Getting it out of your head and expressing it decontaminates your brain.
- Packing a kitchen, closet, garage, etc. often takes longer than other areas, especially when you take the time to pack things as carefully as they ought to be. (I'll talk more about planning in the next chapter.)
  - To avoid becoming physically exhausted – and risking injury – take a five- to ten-minute break each hour and stretch.
    - When you exhaust yourself, stress becomes magnified, and it becomes difficult to make wise decisions.

Do as I Say, Not as I Did

- Actively monitor and manage negative feelings so you can avoid inflicting them on others. Those around you will be grateful and, in the end, so will you.
- When worries start dragging you down, take a break and do something you enjoy, like taking a walk to lift your spirits.
- Go outside and get some fresh air, especially when emotions are at full throttle.

- Talk about these fraught sensations within you with someone you trust – and who's not involved in the move.
- Remember to breathe, as well as use your stomach and thigh muscles to lift heavy things.
- Better yet, ask someone to assist you.
- You can't do everything and you can't do it all alone, so accept help from those you trust, and don't be shy about asking for it.
- Cherish one another.

Every move is unique, and parental moves become vivid stories in the life of a family. As in all narratives, intense emotions can pop up at any time, like whack-a-mole. Conflict will happen.

Use these methods to staunch familial conflicts and other stressors, and use the tools and techniques in the rest of these pages to chug steadily down your track. Your nerves will thank you, and perhaps others will as well.

Now let's get moving!

---

1 "Aging Readiness & Competitiveness / United States," AARP International, 2025, https://www.aarpinternational.org/initiatives/aging-readiness-competitiveness-arc/united-states.

2 "America is Getting Older," United States Census Bureau, June 22, 2023, https://www.census.gov/newsroom/press-releases/2023/population-estimates-characteristics.html.

3 "The Sandwich Generation," Starting Early Newsletter, The Burke Foundation, May 31, 2024, https://newsletter.burkefoundation.org/2024/05/31/the-sandwich-generation/.

4 Denise Wallace et al., "The Social Readjustment Rating Scale: Updated and Modernised," PLOS One, December 18, 2023, https://journals.plos.org/plosone/article?id=10.1371/journal.pone.0295943.

5 If anyone gets sick, pull out those masks left over from the pandemic and make sure everyone wears them.

Move Management Checklist

Done	Task/Subtask	Your Notes
	As soon as you begin contemplating a move:	
☐	Review Service Providers List	
☐	Make a list of moving companies to contact	
☐	Begin sorting and downsizing	

Done	Task/Subtask	Your Notes
	As soon as you know where your parents are moving to – or 8 weeks before Move Day:	
☐	Interview and choose a moving company	
☐	Choose a date for Move Day	
☐	Contact estate sales and/or auction companies	
☐	Find out about permits, regulations, and parking restrictions	

Done	Task/Subtask	Your Notes
☐	Compile "Change of Address" list	
	If the new home will be in a senior living community, condo, apartment (see end of list for additional tasks for senior living communities):	
☐	Get the floor plan / schematic	
☐	Go to the future home and take photos and measurements for the floor plan. *(See Floor Planning Checklist at the end of the next chapter.)*	

Done	Task/Subtask	Your Notes
☐	Begin creating the Floor Plan	
☐	Ask about requirements related to your Move Day (elevator access, time windows, parking, etc.)	
☐	Find out whether the community will handle hooking up the landline phone, cable, and/or internet	
☐	Find out whether the community provides someone who'll hang artwork, photos, and/or wall-mounted TV(s)	

Done	Task/Subtask	Your Notes
	At least one month before Move Day:	
☐	Fill out Change of Address List	
☐	Determine where to store your packed boxes	
☐	Begin packing rarely used items for move	
☐	Determine placement of furniture in new home	

Done	Task/Subtask	Your Notes
	2 weeks before Move Day:	
☐	Find and hire a handyman, if needed	
☐	Secure any permits that you may need	
☐	Make Move Day plan for pets (if any)	
	7 - 10 days before Move Day:	
☐	Alert the moving company about which items they will pack for you (if any)	

Done	Task/Subtask	Your Notes
☐	Alert the moving company about any restrictions or regulations they'll need to follow	
☐	Confirm move date and what time moving truck will arrive	
☐	Alert those on the Change of Address List of new address and move date	
☐	Take clear, close-up photos of devices that require multiple plugs (e.g., computers, TV sets) to show what needs to be plugged in where.	

Done	Task/Subtask	Your Notes
	2 days before Move Day:	
☐	Confirm moving truck's arrival	
☐	Confirm insurance choice with moving company	
☐	Remind moving company about which items they will pack	
☐	Designate a tote bag or small suitcase as the Move Day bag or case.	

Done	Task/Subtask	Your Notes
☐	Use masking tape to label the cords and their corresponding plugs for devices that have multiple plugs to make it easier to set up after the move.	
☐	Place "OPEN FIRST" boxes in one area and tape a sign onto the wall above that says "Load these last" so they'll be the first things off the truck at the new home.	
	Day before Move Day:	
☐	Email Floor Plan to moving company	

Done	Task/Subtask	Your Notes
☐	Print out Floor Plan and Packing List copies to carry with you.	
☐	Stage "Open First" and "Last On / First Off" boxes together	
☐	Ready your Move Day bag or small suitcase and determine who will carry it	
☐	Ready cooler or ice packs for medications requiring refrigeration	

On Move Day, use the Move Day Checklist in chapter *Move Day - i.e., Holy CRAP Day*

Create a Plan

It'll Save Time, Money, and Sanity

Moving is a process, not an event.

You may wonder why you should spend the time creating a plan. Surely you can figure things out as you go along because moving is such a straightforward thing – just pack things up, hire a moving company, then unpack things on the other end, right?

It's not. These transitions are always complicated, so taking the time to use the guidelines, tips, and checklists below will save masses of time and aggravation later.

Any move, particularly one in later life, will take longer than you think. The moment your parents consider moving, start crafting a plan. There's nothing "plug and play" when it comes to moving. Each move has its own idiosyncrasies, but knowing how to fend off the arrows of stress can be transformative.

That's because there's one thing you can surely count on: like any of life's milestones, at some point fate will roll its eyes and send things sideways – another reason why you need a plan.

Ideally, you'll travel through the process at a slow jog and steady pace. This way, you'll have some breathing space.

But sometimes it has to be a strenuous sprint because of a sudden ailment or injury. Even then, take the time to plan.

Add the broad range of this guide's checklists to your plan

As with any major undertaking, each detail of this move will matter. Your plan and checklists act as your anchor, keeping you from drifting out to sea, or spending too much time on useless side trips, as you work through the process – thus saving substantial hours and effort.

Surgeons and operating rooms have checklists so they don't leave scalpels in torsos or operate on the wrong knee. Astronauts have them, too, so they don't float out the air lock in their pajamas. Be inspired by them.

> SMART MOVE TIP:
>
> Move managers – as in project managers for your move – exist and can take on all or as many tasks as you'd like related to this transition. (Admittedly, I'm biased because I became one in 2013 and have loved every bit of it.) This profession requires knowledge, efficiency, and compassion. Many of us have gone through this within our own families and understand what a tremendous burden this is, and we have the expertise to alleviate the stress involved.
>
> Make sure you're hiring someone who's a member of the National Association of Senior & Specialty Move Managers (www.NASMM.org) and, ideally, a Certified Senior Move Manager (SMM-C).

Avoid cramming – start preparing ASAP

Accomplishing things early on is satisfying and motivating. So, unless it's an emergency, start your move preparations as soon as possible, rather than putting things off until the week before. Last-minute moves add misery to an already challenging project. For starters:

- Sleep deprivation and destructive family fights usually occur.

- Expenses can rocket cloud-high, along with your anxiety.

  - Hiring additional people, paying to transport items that no one needs, and the cost of mistakes due to the rush all add up considerably (not to mention you may need to pay for therapy afterward).

The more time you have to plan and knock tasks off your checklist means more time to puzzle out decisions. Then you or someone else can work on the *next* task while you solve that "sideways" problem. Who knows? Your solution might improve on your original idea.

SMART MOVE TIP:

<u>Keep a notebook to keep your sanity</u> – and I mean keep notes on ev-er-y-thing. Every contact, every name, every phone number, every email address. You never know when you'll need it. Moving trucks get flat tires. Rain falls on your estate sale. Your second or third choices may end up riding to the rescue of you and your parents.

I also recommend using a binder to create your own Move Manual. You can slide a spiral notebook in, and a simple three-hole punch so you can easily add all your estimates, contracts, and other information to it.

<u>Notebook tips</u>: Every night, do a "brain dump" to cleanse your thoughts of details you worry you'll forget, so that when you wake up with your heart jumping at 3am, you'll know you've written down all those particulars.

Tuck in any useful new thoughts and ideas that appear in your dreams.

You can record all of this online, but mind who you share your e-notebook with, because someone might delete something vital.

Tasks to Begin Early in the Process

Many tasks can be taken care of early on. Here are three of them:

1. Regulations and Permits

Check on the following requirements for both where you're moving from and where you're moving to:

- Do you need to provide advance notice to reserve parking in front of an apartment or condominium complex?

- If you need permits or orange cones, figure out how to obtain these ahead of time. See if there are any parking restrictions on the street.

- Some buildings have strict regulations about when you can begin or end a move, as well as which elevator you can use. Be sure to ask about them.

Alert the moving company you hire about any and all of these restrictions.

2. Change of Address List

Ahead of move day, make a list of who needs to be notified about your parents' change of address. While you should wait until a week or so before your move to alert everyone, you can create that list now and save time later. You'll want to include:

- Friends and relatives
- Utility bills
- Magazine subscriptions

- Doctors' offices
- Organizations they belong to
- Etc.

I've included a checklist at the end of this chapter so you can keep track of whom to inform.

3. Floor Planning

As soon as you know where your parents are moving to – particularly when it's to a senior living community – ask your liaison there to email a layout or schematic for the apartment they'll be moving into.

Once you have that in hand, go to their new home to explore it. You'll glean answers to these important questions when you visit:

- How big and how many built-in drawers are in the closet(s), kitchen/kitchenette, and/or bathroom?

- Are there any overhead lights? (Knowing this will determine where lamps should go to provide sufficient lighting.)

- How many rungs are in the closet and how big is it?

- Where are the internet and cable hookups?

While you're there, take accurate measurements of each room and area because the floor plan you receive will only be a *template* for all rooms similar to your parents'. The specific measurements may not be precise or obvious on the diagram. Usually, the template doesn't account for the corner where you lose a square foot or so because, in that tiny area, they've walled up some plumbing or duct work. Some people who *really* like their possessions have precise plans for every square foot. Discovering something can't fit on Move Day creates disruption and, possibly, an eruption.

You, your parents, and your movers will be *so* grateful to have this floor plan on Move Day. You can indicate on the floor plan where you want each box and piece of furniture placed. Granted, there's always some tweaking involved. But this plan will save you hours of time, surrounded by annoyed movers, as your parents figure out where they want things. (And if you're paying by the hour, it adds up.)

4. List of Who Can Help

Which professionals will you need to hire? Which friends and relatives can you call on for support? For that latter list, add anyone who owes you or your parents a favor at the top of it.

Wondering how to determine who's the right fit for both lists? Since these people will all be coming into your parents' home to handle all their treasures and belongings, consider them carefully.

MOVING MOMENTS

We worked with a delightful couple in their 70s who were moving from a stately home. Lynn and I had both graduated from the same university. Her husband Stan had Parkinson's Disease, unfortunately, and they were moving to an assisted living community for his benefit.

My colleagues enjoyed working with them and had been making steady progress for weeks. Their Move Day was approaching.

I walked into my office one morning and found that Lynn had left a voicemail at about 8 am. Desolation engulfed her voice. Stan had passed away overnight. Even though he'd died just a few hours before, she said she had to let us know because, "You're family."

I was thankful I had a box of tissues on my desk as I dialed her number.

My colleagues were sorrowful and dumbfounded by this news. Aghast, one of them said, "I was just working with him yesterday afternoon."

Floor Planning Checklist

Done	Task/Subtask	Your Notes
☐	Get a floor plan for the new home.	
☐	Schedule a time to go measure the new home.	
☐	Take photos and/or video of rooms and areas	
☐	Measure all rooms and areas	

Done	Task/Subtask	Your Notes
☐	Record *length*, *width*, AND *height* of each room / area	
☐	Measure *height from floor to bottom of each window* (in case you want to place furniture there).	
☐	**Measure closet space. Note the number of:**	
☐	Rungs, and/or	
☐	Shelves	

Done	Task/Subtask	Your Notes
☐	**In the bathroom: Note the number of:**	
☐	Drawers and/or cabinets (including medicine cabinet)	
☐	**In the kitchen/kitchenette: Note the number of:**	
☐	Drawers	
☐	Cabinets	
☐	Shelves (including those within cabinets)	

Done	Task/Subtask	Your Notes
☐	Counterspace	
☐	**Note locations of the following:**	
☐	Overhead lighting	
☐	Emergency pulls	
☐	Electrical outlets	
☐	Phone outlets	
☐	Cable outlets	

Done	Task/Subtask	Your Notes
☐	Internet outlets	
☐	Heating/Air Conditioning units that jut into the room from the window or are anchored to the floor	
☐	Create a to-scale diagram of the new home using graph paper, a spreadsheet, or an app.	
☐	Add a legend/key on the side that indicates what abbreviations stand for (i.e., "E" for electrical outlets, "L" to indicate overhead light, etc.)	

Done	Task/Subtask	Your Notes
☐	Place furniture, keeping flow and function in mind. **Walker or wheelchair access:** Be sure there is at least 36" of clearance in all directions and through doorways so mobility is not hampered.	
☐	Place beds near emergency pulls	
☐	Place TVs near cable outlets and landline phones (if any) near phone outlets	

Done	Task/Subtask	Your Notes
☐	Once Floor Plan has been completed:	
☐	Scan the Floor Plan, then upload and save it on your computer.	
☐	Share the Floor Plan with your parents.	
☐	Print out copies to have them ready for Move Day	

Change of Address List

Done	Who	Email / Website / Addresses / Notes
		Family Members
☐		
☐		
☐		
☐		

Done	Who	Email / Website / Addresses / Notes
☐		
☐		
☐		
☐		
☐		

Done	Who	Email / Website / Addresses / Notes
		Subscriptions
☐		
☐		
☐		
☐		
☐		

Done	Who	Email / Website / Addresses / Notes
☐		
☐		
☐		
☐		
☐		

Done	Who	Email / Website / Addresses / Notes
	Financial Accounts (Bank, Credit Cards, Loans, 401k's, Investment, etc.)	
☐	Bank(s)	
☐	Credit Card(s)	
☐	Investment / IRA	
☐	401k / Pension Plan	
☐	Mortgage	

Done	Who	Email / Website / Addresses / Notes
☐	Car Loan	
☐		
☐		
☐		
☐		
☐		

Done	Who	Email / Website / Addresses / Notes
		Utilities
☐	Electricity	
☐	Water	
☐	Gas	
☐	Cable TV	
☐	Internet Provider	

Done	Who	Email / Website / Addresses / Notes
☐	Phone(s)	
☐		
☐		
	Doctors	
☐		
☐		

Done	Who	Email / Website / Addresses / Notes
☐		
☐		
☐		
☐		
☐		
☐		

Done	Who	Email / Website / Addresses / Notes
	Professionals	
☐	Attorney - Estate Planning	
☐	Accountant	
☐		
☐		
☐		

Done	Who	Email / Website / Addresses / Notes
	Government Agencies	
☐	Voter Registration	
☐	Dept. of Motor Vehicles (Driver's License)	
☐	Social Security Administration	
☐		
☐		

Done	Who	Email / Website / Addresses / Notes
☐		
	Friends / Neighbors	
☐		
☐		
☐		
☐		

Done	Who	Email / Website / Addresses / Notes
☐		
☐		
☐		
☐		
☐		
☐		

Done	Who	Email / Website / Addresses / Notes
☐		
☐		
☐		
☐		
☐		
☐		

Done	Who	Email / Website / Addresses / Notes
		Others to Notify
☐		
☐		
☐		
☐		
☐		

Done	Who	Email / Website / Addresses / Notes
☐		
☐		
☐		
☐		
☐		
☐		

Who Can (and Really Will) Help You for Free

I believe that most of us want to feel useful to others (or at least have others think we are), so you may be gladdened by how many friends, relatives, and neighbors nod enthusiastically when you ask them for help. Embrace these offers of assistance and, simultaneously, corral your expectations.

While your friendly volunteers are all well-intentioned, be realistic about who will show up, and how much they will *really* get done. Most importantly, they're not professionals who do this sort of thing day in and day out. Many will unintentionally overstate how much they can help you.

Dependability may vary. People will come late, leave early, get tired, or complain about some muscle ache or another. Sometimes they'll simply say, "something came up." No matter the lament, be merciful since we've all said that at one time or another.

Those who *do* show up for you deserve to be celebrated. Provide snacks and sodas aplenty while you all work. At the end of the day, serve up delicious food, along with beer and ice cream as rewards.

Also plan for some poorly packed boxes, and possibly a couple of broken items. I strongly suggest compiling some guidelines and packing instructions to share (see the *How to Pack, Label, and Stack Your Stuff* chapter). Perhaps begin the day with a *demonstration* of how you'd like things packed, so no one has to guess, and they'll be less shy about asking questions.

As you all begin to work, say, "I know you'll treat my items as if they were your own, and thank you for that." This graciously reminds them how important these items are to you and your family.

Figure out ahead of time how you'll strike a balance between being their cheerleader and taskmaster. You don't want to scold anyone, stalk off, or just stand there silently and grim-faced. You may already be tired as the day begins, and you certainly will be toward the end of the day.

- Think of a few inoffensive phrases you can use to explain how you'd like things done differently when you see someone handling your fragile items awkwardly.

    ◦ "That thing is so weird and unwieldy. Let me help you with that."

    ◦ "This will be so complicated to pack. Let me help you." Or "Let me take it off your hands. I'll get it packed."

- Kindly re-assign them to a task that doesn't involve anything delicate, like packing your books.

    ◦ "There's a ridiculous amount of books in the other room. Would you mind taking care of those? I can take care of these."

If possible, you could designate a "bad cop" so you can be the "good cop." That, or find a way to be a *mellow* bad cop.

Be generous with your thanks throughout the day, and express appreciation like, "You're doing great!" or "I can't believe you got so much done!"

The next day, send an effusive "thank you" email, and let them know you'll have a housewarming party when everyone and everything settled after the move – and they won't need to raise a finger.

SMART MOVE TIP:

When you have help from friends, family members, or others who don't pack for a living, it's a good idea to check the first few boxes (at least) to be sure your belongings are packed safely - even if you've provided a live demonstration beforehand.

So neither you nor they feel like you're hovering, put a box down next to them and pack other items while they pack theirs. If they have questions or need help, you're right there.

Hiring Help & How to Do It

Think of paying for professional help (move managers, financial advisors, etc.) as a worthy investment. It's daunting, and sometimes fear-inducing, to entrust prized belongings, or your parents' legal and financial needs, to paid professionals who are new to you. You wonder if they'll somehow cheat your parents, not respond when they break the leg of an heirloom chair, or when a substantial sum slips from a bank account unexpectedly.

If you think you "ought to" be managing everything for them, think about these reasons for employing outside assistance:

- Many parents don't want to ask their adult offspring for help. It can feel like a hit to their pride and independence.

- Parents don't want to be a burden to any of their grown children. They recognize your life may already be on overload managing a full-time career, raising your own children, and/or living far afield.

- If you're contending with back pain, knee problems, or hands besieged by carpal tunnel syndrome, parents worry about that, too.

- Parents and their adult children - no matter how much they love each other - butt horns at a time like this. Guaranteed.

- I've often had to remind fully-grown kids that, "Your parents remember changing your diapers," so of course they "know better." What could you possibly know that they don't?

Case in point: I vividly recall sitting in a doctor's office with my father, and hearing that doctor tell him exactly the same thing I had told my dad time and time again. Whenever I had said it, my father always dismissed the idea in a way that struck me, his youngest daughter, as condescending.

When that doctor repeated what I had been trying to get past his "father filter" for so long, Dad brightened as if similar words had never entered his ears before and said, "Oh, that's a great idea!"

Sound familiar?

That doctor was a hired expert. The same thing can happen when you hire other professionals. We can parrot what you've expressed a hundred times over, and your parents may well react as if they've never heard those words before.

A professional you've hired isn't a family member and can therefore often convince your parents to consider the point you've been making. We serve as the external expert, and a neutral one at that (theoretically, anyhow), and everyone wants to be rewarded for their good performance.

That's why specialists like me can get your dad to surrender thirteen of his fifteen hammers – and you can't. I'm often grateful for this predictable behavior, as sometimes it's the only way to move a project forward.

> ## INSIDE SCOOP
>
> I love science, and that includes psychology. When quarreling sides shift to good behavior when a new onlooker joins them, there's a name for that: Self-Presentation Theory, something first written about by Canadian sociologist Erving Goffman in his 1956 book, *The Presentation of Self in Everyday Life*[6]. I think a sprinkling of the Audience Effect[7] is also involved. The larger theory of social facilitation – when people perform better when in the presence of others - envelopes both these theories and others and was first identified back in 1898 by American psychologist Norman Triplett.[8] (I can descend deep, deep down the rabbit hole when examining human behavior, which is as multi-hued as a meadow's flowers, but also more intricate and unyielding than the Gordian Knot.)

Hiring support like move managers and financial advisors benefits you and your parents in so many other ways, too:

- We know what catastrophes can happen, how to prevent them, and how to manage them if they do happen.
- You won't need to take a week off from work to do something efficient service providers can do in a day.
- You'll get more sleep because you have experts handling the tough stuff.

Finding and Vetting Trustworthy Professionals

But how do you find trustworthy and dependable people? If you're already working with someone you trust, such as an estate planning attorney or realtor, ask them if they can provide recommendations to you. Most of us have a list of such partners and refer them with careful consideration. Whomever I recommend has already done excellent work for our clients or other partners. I know my reputation is on the line as much as theirs.

Interview at least two of each profession and, no matter how good they look online or how highly recommended they come, do your due diligence.

Below is a list of questions to ask any professional you're considering. Listen closely to their answers and ask them additional questions until you feel fully informed:

- How many years has the company been in business with the current owner?
    - Moving companies and home care companies are often bought and sold over the years. Then new management takes over, which may be better or worse than the previous owners.
- Is the company insured for:
    - Liability
    - Errors & Omissions
    - Workers Compensation

- Are they a member of their national trade association, and are they in good standing with that organization?
  - Check the association's website for a list of current members or call them.
- What licenses, certifications, and/or education do they have?
- If you'll be assigned someone to work with from the company, will they be an employee or independent contractor?
  - Employees are ideal. If they're independent contractors, they may lack specialized training and probably aren't insured by the company you hired.
- Will the company you're considering provide references?

Be even more diligent when interviewing moving companies

When you're hiring a moving company, here are some important additional questions to ask:

- Will they provide a Certificate of Insurance (COI) for you?
  - A COI for moving provides proof of liability insurance to make sure the structure of the house or building – such as elevators, walls, and floors - is insured, in case of any damage.
  - This may be especially important if you're moving from, or into, a condo or apartment complex, or a senior living community, as the company that owns the building may require it.

- Will they provide their Department of Transportation license number?

    ◦ If they don't have one, they're not legitimate. Walk away immediately.

- What do they unpack?
- Will they remove the empty boxes and moving materials once things are unpacked?
- Do they have a "summer surcharge"?

    ◦ The busiest time by far for movers is between Memorial Day weekend and Labor Day weekend, so make plans with them well in advance – two to three months ahead - if you plan to move during the summer months. Plan ahead.

    ◦ For a move out of the area, movers tack on an extra fee during those months. If it's a local move, they normally charge their regular rates, but make sure to ask.

- If you're planning a long-distance move, approximately how long will the moving truck take to arrive at your parents' new home?

    ◦ Long-distance moving trucks are huge. Many of our clients moves have been considered only a "partial load," meaning that their items will be stored until they have a sufficient amount from other moves to fill up their very large truck.

    ◦ This is standard practice and it means that it could be a few days or a week before they get on the road.

    ◦ Initially, the moving company will provide you with a delivery window of about four to seven days. That delivery window will shrink as the moving truck gets closer to the destination.

- Will your items stay on the same truck the whole way or will they be transferred to another truck at some point for transport?
    - Any time your items are shifted from one vehicle to the next, there's the risk of damage to your items.
    - One truck is ideal but, when it's long-distance, your possessions may be moved to at least one other truck.
- What kind of insurance coverage do they provide for lost or damaged items?
    - The standard insurance provided by moving companies currently only pays out 60 cents ($0.60) per pound if something is lost or damaged. (You read that right – 6 dimes for each pound lost or damaged.)
    - If you want any additional insurance, you'll need to pay for that, so find out about their rates for better coverage.
- Are they a full-fledged moving company or are they a moving broker?

Getting Estimates

If you're moving out of your local area with a substantial amount of furniture and items, most moving companies will visit the home and provide free estimates. For local moves, that's not usually the case but, thanks to technology, you can do a virtual walk-through so the movers see all that they'll be contending with, such as stairways, narrow hallways, or bringing items down from an attic. They can then put together an estimate for you.

> ### INSIDE SCOOP
>
> During the COVID-19 pandemic, a colleague was moving from Los Angeles to Denver. I asked her which moving company she and her husband had selected. Turns out I had never heard of the company they'd hired. Their move was imminent but I asked her to run the questions above by this company.
>
> When she called them, they hung up after she asked about their insurance coverage.
>
> Fortunately, I know many moving companies who've done great work for our clients, and I provided her with three recommendations. The one she and her husband chose worked out well for them.

Work with a moving company – not a moving broker

A bonafide moving company takes care of your move from start to finish, but a broker sells your contract to a moving company you may or may not have heard of. The regulators (Federal Motor Carrier Safety Administration) state it best[9]: "A moving broker is a company that arranges for the transportation of your cargo, utilizing for-hire carriers to provide the actual truck transportation. Moving brokers are sales teams that book your move and sell it to an actual moving company."

HOW TO MOVE YOUR PARENTS

"A moving broker is not a mover. A broker does not assume responsibility for, and is not authorized to transport, your household goods. Brokers do not have moving trucks or professional movers. Brokers for interstate moves are required to use only movers that are registered with FMCSA."

"Sometimes the broker is not able to sell the job to a moving company for various reasons – low estimates, no availability, limited resources, etc. – and in this case you can get stuck without a mover on the day of your move. Many moving brokers operate from call centers located anywhere in the country."

As I said, hire a moving *company* that actually moves your possessions from one place to another, and will take responsibility for them.

One last point: <u>Do not hire on the spot</u>. Take at least one day to consider your decision. Sleep on it - literally. And then get everything in writing.

---

6 Adam D. Barnhart, "Erving Goffman: The Presentation of Self in Everyday Life," Portland State University, accessed January 31, 2025, https://web.pdx.edu/~tothm/theory/Presentation%20of%20Self.htm.

7 Antonia F. de C. Hamilton, Frida: "Audience effects: what can they tell us about social neuroscience, theory of mind and autism?," Culture and Brain 4 (2016), 159–177, https://doi.org/10.1007/s40167-016-0044-5.

8 Allison Wallace, "An Extension of Social Facilitation Theory to the Decision-Making Domain," All Theses 1258 (2011), 2-9, https://tigerprints.clemson.edu/all_theses/1258.

9 "Movers vs. Brokers," Federal Motor Carrier Safety Administration, U.S. Department of Transportation, last updated November 4, 2024, https://www.fmcsa.dot.gov/protect-your-move/movers-vs-brokers.

Professionals & Services to Consider

This is a list of professionals and services that you may want to consider contacting to assist you and your parents.

Done	Who	Email / Website / Addresses / Notes
☐	Accountant (C.P.A.)	
☐	Appraiser	
☐	Attorney – Estate Planning	
☐	Attorney - Taxes	
☐	Auto Transport	

Done	Who	Email / Website / Addresses / Notes
☐	Care Manager	
☐	Caregivers	
☐	Cleaning Service	
☐	Closet Designers (for built-ins)	
☐	Computer installation, hook-up, or repair	
☐	Contractor	

Done	Who	Email / Website / Addresses / Notes
☐	Donation Organizations	
☐	Electrician	
☐	Estate Sales and/or Auction Companies	
☐	Financial Advisor	
☐	Handyman	
☐	Haul Away	

Done	Who	Email / Website / Addresses / Notes	
☐	Insurance Broker		
☐	Interior Decorator		
☐	Moving & Transportation Companies		
☐	Move Manager		
☐	Photo Digitizing		
☐	Plumber		

Done	Who	Email / Website / Addresses / Notes
☐	Realtor	
☐	Senior Residential Placement Agency	
☐	Shredding of Documents	
☐	Stager	

Mental Maintenance: How to Keep Your Head from Exploding

Wise decisions require alert and supple brain circuitry. Stress, however, from the continual stream of choices involved with a move can potentially melt your gray matter. If you weren't grinding your teeth before, you probably are now.

When your brain feels determined to burst through your skull:

- Smile. Science proves it makes you feel better.
- Try the Superman stance for the same effect.
    - Take a few minutes to check out from the task in front of you and check in with your senses.
    - Turn your phone off.
    - Have a seat and rest your feet on the floor.
    - Close your eyes.
    - Listen only to your inhales and exhales.[10]

Any of these will pull you into the moment and clear your head a bit. I advise you to do this before you begin the sorting and downsizing process. Each item could become a landmine that injures the bond between you and your parents, so tread carefully.

They may cling to heirlooms or want them to at least stay in the family – which is why they want to give you two generations' worth of china sets, their stamp collection, and the armoire that hasn't been shellacked in 90 years.

All jesting aside, your parents' history may contain two of the greatest tragedies of the twentieth century: World War II and the Great Depression. They may have endured one or both of these catastrophic events, or they may have been born during their unsteady aftermath. Either way, they inherited their parents' trauma.

I refer to those people from this time as the "Deprivation Generation" because of all they had to do without, my own parents among them. The 1930s and 1940s were perilous times that scratched out trenches of despair in people's hearts and memories. They were taught that everything had value and needed to be kept. They also were not allowed to be a burden, especially to their families.

Please don't discount these feelings. Ask them to tell you their stories, even if you've heard them all your life. It's easier to let go of something once they're sure its story has been heard. Taking a few photos sometimes helps. Maybe record a video of them telling you the story, so you can save it for future generations.

As challenging as this process may become, their vibrant lives deserve recognition and remembrance. Be patient as you collaborate with them to find those treasures that merit keeping.

---

10 You'll notice I didn't say to meditate regularly. Since I rarely do so myself, I'd be an awful hypocrite to recommend it.

Tackling the Acreage of Memories

Does your moving project seem like a nebulous glob you can't quite grasp? If so, you are not alone, but now you're about to get your arms around it.

THE most important thing to know is that you need to break down this project into easily digestible steps. You wouldn't eat a Thanksgiving feast in one gulp, right? It's one course, one bite at a time. And each part of your scrumptious meal is made from a recipe of individual ingredients that, once combined, collectively delight your tastebuds.

Breaking it Down

For your feast – the move – the individual elements will be the tasks and subtasks required. One of the first tasks that may have come to mind is packing. As it turns out, before you get to packing, you need to accomplish the following tasks:

- Sorting and downsizing
- Choosing what's moving with you
- Setting aside all that isn't
- Buying packing supplies

Then, you'll need to break down each of these tasks into subtasks. Let's take sorting and downsizing. Begin by breaking this down by rooms:

- Main bedroom
- Guest bedroom
- Living room
- Dining area
- Kitchen
- Garage
- Attic, etc.

Let's say your parents' main bedroom includes the area holding the bed and other furniture, a bathroom, and a walk-in closet. You can further dissect areas like these into additional subtasks.

By now, you can appreciate why you want to start preparing for your parents' Move Day as soon as possible, even if it's a year away. The more time you have, the more you can spread out what you need to do, and that will keep anxiety to a minimum.

Limits are Your Friends

This is a marathon, not a 5K, and you need to pace yourself.

When you begin your sorting and downsizing process, I highly recommend setting either a time limit or a space limit (as in limiting your work to a small and specific area).

If you choose a time limit, start with one hour. Once that hour has passed, you get to stop for the day. Or, with a space limit, keep your first session focused on a single kitchen cabinet. When the cabinet's been sorted, that session's over.

Use your calendar to keep you on track. There's an Action Plan at the end of this chapter that helps break this all down for you.

You'll save time and effort – and ensure you don't miss any tasks – by scheduling times on your calendar when you'll take on each area and subtask. You may need to move some around, but you've now framed a structure for yourself.

As you progress, you can certainly extend it to two hours per session or take on additional kitchen cabinets. Just make sure that each session's assignment feels achievable, especially in the beginning.

Also, make it enjoyable! Play music that makes you move. Have your favorite snacks and beverages nearby and, when your work for that day is done, celebrate by checking off one more item on your list.

INSIDE SCOOP

I have a dear friend back in my hometown of Buffalo whom I'll call Marie. Several years ago, she was going through a very difficult divorce and her soon-to-be-ex-husband still lived in the home they had shared for many years. One of their daughters still lived there, too.

Marie had moved out but still needed to clear her clothes and other things from their shared closet. But she could not get herself to do it, even when her almost-ex-husband wasn't home.

Fortunately, she picked up her daughter from high school every day and drove her to that house. Her nearly-ex-husband didn't come home until an hour or more after that, so she could put this pocket of time to use.

I explained this idea of using a time limit to pull her clothing out, one day at a time. She started spending twenty minutes during each visit to liberate her things from that closet. It wasn't long before it became her ex-closet.

Bit by bit, piece by piece, memory by memory. That's how to get it done.

Sorting & Downsizing Action Plan

How to Use Your Sorting & Downsizing Action Plan:

- On the first column on the left side, list the three rooms or areas that intimidate you the most.

- In the second column, write down three problem spots to tackle in each of these rooms. (In my living room, these are my coffee table, alcove, and bookcase. Yes, clutter collects in my home, too. It's so much easier tackling some else's clutter!)

- In the third column, add the date and time you'll tackle these areas, along with a name if someone's coming to support you.

Done	Room *(Main Bedroom, Garage, Patio, Yard Shed, etc.)*	Area *(Nightstands, Upper right cabinet, Closet rung, etc.)*	Date & Time / Notes *(Sat. 2/28 1pm - Susan & Nigel to help; buy trash bags, sodas & chocolate)*
☐			
☐			
☐			
☐			
☐			

Done	Room *(Main Bedroom, Garage, Patio, Yard Shed, etc.)*	Area *(Nightstands, Upper right cabinet, Closet rung, etc.)*	Date & Time / Notes *(Sat. 2/28 1pm - Susan & Nigel to help; buy trash bags, sodas & chocolate)*
☐			
☐			
☐			
☐			

Done	Room (Main Bedroom, Garage, Patio, Yard Shed, etc.)	Area (Nightstands, Upper right cabinet, Closet rung, etc.)	Date & Time / Notes (Sat. 2/28 1pm - Susan & Nigel to help; buy trash bags, sodas & chocolate)
☐			
☐			
☐			
☐			
☐			

Done	Room *(Main Bedroom, Garage, Patio, Yard Shed, etc.)*	Area *(Nightstands, Upper right cabinet, Closet rung, etc.)*	Date & Time / Notes *(Sat. 2/28 1pm - Susan & Nigel to help; buy trash bags, sodas & chocolate)*
☐			
☐			
☐			
☐			

Done	Room (Main Bedroom, Garage, Patio, Yard Shed, etc.)	Area (Nightstands, Upper right cabinet, Closet rung, etc.)	Date & Time / Notes (Sat. 2/28 1pm - Susan & Nigel to help; buy trash bags, sodas & chocolate)
☐			
☐			
☐			
☐			
☐			

Done	Room *(Main Bedroom, Garage, Patio, Yard Shed, etc.)*	Area *(Nightstands, Upper right cabinet, Closet rung, etc.)*	Date & Time / Notes *(Sat. 2/28 1pm - Susan & Nigel to help; buy trash bags, sodas & chocolate)*
☐			
☐			
☐			
☐			

Done	Room (Main Bedroom, Garage, Patio, Yard Shed, etc.)	Area (Nightstands, Upper right cabinet, Closet rung, etc.)	Date & Time / Notes (Sat. 2/28 1pm - Susan & Nigel to help; buy trash bags, sodas & chocolate)
☐			
☐			
☐			
☐			
☐			

Safety is Everyone's Responsibility

The "emotional flu" is one thing. Breaking your actual ankle or another bone is something much more intrusive and thrusts you to the sidelines. Or what if your parent falls and winds up with 23 stitches after slicing an arm with a box cutter?

For many reasons, nursing a bodily injury is the last thing you want added to your overflowing platter. Providing a safe environment for you and your family protects everyone involved with this move. Setting up safety precautions is a must-do, so bruises, blood, and strained muscles don't materialize.

11 Vital Safety Rules

You'll find a quick checklist of these at the end of this chapter, but listed here are the reasons why they're necessary. (Send the checklist ahead of time to those working with you, so they understand and adhere to these guidelines.)

1. What to Wear – and not to Wear

Alert the friends and family members who plan to assist you about these important details so they come prepared.

Make sure everyone – including you - wears clothes no one will mind tearing, snagging, or staining. *Sturdy, closed-toe shoes* are another must - *no flip flops and no bare feet.* Otherwise, you could slice a foot, or even sprain or break toes. You might step on or bump into something, or have a bookshelf dropped on your foot, which is its own singular hell.

I know that all sounds gruesome, but these things happen.

Don't forget your safety gear! Keep gloves – both disposable and thicker cloth ones – at the ready. You'd be amazed at what can invade your fingernails or, worse, draw blood. Have dust masks and shoe booties standing by, too, especially when you're working in the garage, an outdoor shed or attic. You probably have some left over from the pandemic, so put them to use.

2. Bending and Lifting

There's a whole lot of bending and lifting to do when you're sorting, packing, and unpacking. This is not the time for machismo or showing off, unless you want a strained back or herniated discs, so know and respect how much is safe for you to lift and carry.

Remember to bend your knees when lifting and to engage your abdominal muscles, and request help for weighty or unwieldy items or boxes.

3. Circulation Paths and Keeping Floors Clear of Sorted Items

There will be days when your work in an area is incomplete, but it's time to call it a day and leave things as they are. Sometimes that can be in a very busy area, and you don't want anyone (especially a parent) tripping over packing materials or sorted items.

Falls are a huge risk factor for everyone, especially older adults. As exhausted as you may be after all your sorting and downsizing, it's important that you make sure all floors are kept clear of anything that could cause a fall or injury.

For everyone's sake, before you stop work for the day, organize everything on one side, making sure there's a pathway that's at least 36 inches wide. This can be a challenge when rooms are full of boxes, but it's *very* important if someone uses a cane or walker and risks stepping on the cutting edge of a tape gun or other sharp object.

4. Area and Throw Rugs

Any loose rugs should come with neon-lit "TRIP HAZARD" signs. Roll them up and stash them in a garage or large closet as you prepare to move so no one catches a shoe, toe, or walker leg in one of them and takes a bad fall. Better yet, banish them from the house entirely.

If you can't talk your parents out of moving loose rugs to their new home, be sure to secure them in place with double-sided rug tape or a non-slip mat underneath.

5. Electrical Hazards

Electrical cords are useful – and *dangerous*. Add an accidental spark from an electrical wire to the mix, and things can go up in flames. And that peril is in addition to the threat of trips and falls.

See any frayed electrical cords? *Do not plug those in anywhere.* They are incredibly dangerous! Besides the risk of sparks, a bare live cord touched by someone with a pacemaker can send them to the hospital. Far better to repair, trash, or recycle what that frayed cord is attached to so it's no longer a danger.

6. Stepladders

At some point, you'll need to tackle those high corners of the closets, the top shelves in the kitchen, and any other spot requiring a ladder.

Step stools and stepladders vary widely in height and stability. Test them with one foot on the bottom rung first, making sure there's no shaking and that it doesn't feel flimsy or out of balance.

Even when that step stool or ladder feels steady and secure, it's best to have someone standing on the floor behind you to support you should anything happen, particularly when you're stretching deep into closet corners, reaching into tall kitchen cupboards, or handling anything heavy.

7. Attic and Basement Stairs

When you're going up into an attic or down into a basement or cellar, you need sturdy stairs and plenty of light. If you happen upon a burn-out bulb, replace it on the spot. Also have a flashlight at the ready and move slowly and carefully – or keep both hands free by strapping on a headlamp.

Attics often come with the challenge of climbing Bessler (drop-down) stairs. We had these in our family home. Even when I was young and felt indestructible, I found them unnerving. Always have someone working with you when dealing with Bessler stairs to keep you safe as you shift things up and down from the attic.

8. Pets

Non-human members of your family need to be kept safe and sound, too. Stress is contagious and your pets are not immune, so keep in mind they may behave unpredictably, just as humans do when we're anxious.

Doors will be opened and shut repeatedly while you're working in different rooms and areas. Pets can easily escape, slide under your feet, or hide in places where no one can find them.

While everyone else is sorting and organizing, nestle your pets in a room other than the one you're working in. Provide them with a water bowl and perhaps turn a radio on so it sounds to them like they have company.

On Move Day, if you can, take them to a friend's home, place them in a carrier or treat them to doggie day care. They'll be more comfortable, and so will you. Think of the exciting reunion they'll have with your parents in their new home.

As things are moved around, a lot of dust gets kicked up, and this may affect pets with allergies. Sometimes the litter box or a very lived-in birdcage gets bumped and all kinds of nasty goes flying. Make sure to wash your hands thoroughly and frequently.

9. Working with Dementia

If dementia has taken hold of your parent, they can become increasingly agitated, even physically aggressive, when they see you disturbing their belongings. As you sort and downsize rooms, ask a friend or family member to take them out for an excursion, or to at least keep them out of the room so they won't be upset by all the activity.

10. First Aid, Germs, and Illness Prevention

Dig out your first aid kit and latex gloves. Wear the gloves and wash your hands when working anywhere that germs, bacteria, and other invasive and nasty things lurk, such as bathrooms. Keep this kit handy, as antibacterial ointment and bandages of various sizes may be needed.

Since cuts and scratches, however minor, are a possibility, consider getting a tetanus shot. Once you've had an initial tetanus shot, you should get one every ten years.[11]

Ask anyone who has the sniffles, itchy throat, or the tummy rumbles, to stay home and rest. If they insist on coming, have them wear a mask and gloves. That also goes for those who suffer from dust allergies.

11. Pointy Things

That first aid kit is often opened due to unpleasant encounters with sharp objects. Let's avoid those, shall we?

HOW TO MOVE YOUR PARENTS

Leave kitchen knives either in a knife block or secreted in drawers until it's time to pack them. (You'll find specific instructions about how to pack knives in the *How to Pack, Label, and Stack Your Stuff Like a Pro* chapter.)

Keep box cutters and utility knives retracted when not in use. If you lend some to those helping you, count the ones you give out, and count those returned. If those numbers don't match, keep looking.

By following these guidelines, everyone will be prepared, aware, and alert. Lessening or, better yet, eliminating injuries and illness keeps the move moving forward.

---

11 Pritish K. Tosh, "Tetanus shots: Is it risky to receive 'extra' boosters?," Mayo Clinic, July 27, 2023, https://www.mayoclinic.org/diseases-conditions/tetanus/expert-answers/tetanus-shots/faq-20058209.

Safety Checklist

Send this out ahead of time so anyone who comes to help will be prepared.

Please be aware of these guidelines so that everyone's protected.

What to wear:	Why?
Closed-toe, comfortable shoes. No flip flops.	Keep your toes safe!
Clothing that can get dirty and/or snagged.	Just in case.
Bring thick gloves if you have them.	I've got plenty of latex gloves for you to use.
Things to be aware of ahead of time:	
The limit of what you can carry.	Don't overdo it! Ask for help.
If you have a cold, flu, or anything contagious, please stay at home. Take care of yourself and rest. I know you'll be with us in spirit.	

What to wear:	Why?
If you have dust allergies and plan on coming, ask me for a mask so you don't wind up miserable.	There'll also be tissues in case you need them.
Safety guidelines to follow:	
Keep circulation paths clear of debris and items to pack.	We don't want anyone tripping or falling.
Use stepladders for higher shelves - and have someone standing beside you in case something throws you off balance.	Same as above.
If an overhead light somewhere isn't working, please let me know so I can replace it for you.	I also have a flashlight if you need one.
Our [mom's / dad's / parents'] [pet(s)] will be in the main bedroom with the door closed while we're all working.	[Pet's name] might get too excited and run out the door, or trip on something. This way, they're safe.

What to wear:	**Why?**
Additional important things to know:	
We have a first-aid kit standing by. If you cut yourself, please let me know so we can get you bandaged up.	Better yet, be super careful so you don't get injured!
Water, sodas, and snacks will be available in the kitchen all day long. Please enjoy them!	We'll order [food, e.g., pizza] toward the end, and I'd love it if you'd stay and enjoy it with us!

Act Two

Time to Dig In – But Where?

What seems to overwhelm people most when they're staring at a room full of clutter is the totality of it, the *gestalt*, meaning "an organized whole that is perceived as more than the sum of its parts."[12]

That's why your moving project needs to be broken down into manageable parts, so you can override this perception and know in your marrow that you can conquer this move.

You have to start somewhere, but where? Over the years, I've walked into many client situations and asked myself the same question, especially when I've faced hoarding conditions.

Top Preparation Tips for Sorting and Downsizing

Approaching this part of the process methodically means you'll have a path to follow even on days when being a zombie would improve your focus. You can still go through the motions and make some headway.

To Begin, Pick a Room

I figured out early in my move management career to just pick a room either at the front or back of the house and walk into it. Once in, I'd choose either the wall directly to my left or the one to my right and begin. Steadily and gradually, I'd work my way around the room. When that room was finished, I'd walk into the one next to it, work my way around in the same way, and then walk into the next.

Use a System

When you tackle the kitchen, you're faced with a series of cupboards and drawers. How do you keep track of which ones have been dealt with?

With any group of drawers, either begin at the top and work your way down, or vice versa. Tackle the cupboards in a similar way by starting on one side of the kitchen or the other and steadily working your way from one to the next. As you start your sorting, begin with the top shelf or the bottom shelf.

If you hop around from one area to another, no matter how big or small, you can't see the steady progress you're making. But you do want to see progress, because it will make your heart blossom to gaze upon the three cabinets you've finished downsizing.

Also, when you have helpers, it's easy to know where and how to direct them, thanks to your easily understood system. You'll always know where things left off and where the next session should begin. Making linear, visual progress will invigorate you even when coffee can't.

Mark Your Progress

Consider placing a small piece of painter's or masking tape on the handles of drawers and cabinets you've gone through. This way, everyone knows which cupboards have been sorted, and that can prevent any clutter creep from retaking them.

Sort now, not later

Occasionally, a client with a last-minute move will tell us to just pack everything and they'll downsize after the move. We have one response to this: "Do you *really* want to pay to move something you're going to toss out afterward?"

Fortunately, you're taking the time to prep properly, which means you'll downsize ahead of time and save money, time, and grief.

---

12 "True or False: Gestalt theory is an organized whole that is perceived as more than the sum of its parts," Brainly, accessed February 1, 2025, https://brainly.com/question/38305892.

The C.L.E.A.N.S.E. Concept

Straightforward Methods to Simplify, Sort, & Downsize

No doubt you want to sort and downsize things as efficiently as possible. Understanding key tenets of organizing will not only move your move along, but it'll also serve you well anywhere that could use some weeding out.

As you begin, keep everyone focused on their <u>favorite and most useful items</u>. (A toothbrush doesn't usually "spark joy," per Marie Kondo, but it is incredibly useful.)

Early in my move-management career, I combined fundamental techniques to create the C.L.E.A.N.S.E. Concept. It breaks down the process we use at Clear Home Solutions in a way that's easy to memorize. Each of these principles applies whether you're preparing for a move or just organizing a file drawer.

Here's a Quick C.L.E.A.N.S.E. Primer:

"C" stands for **CONCENTRATE***:*
    <u>Concentrate</u> on one area and one room at a time.

"L" stands for **LOCALIZE***:*
    <u>Localize</u> items where they're actually used.

"E" stands for **ELIMINATE**:
Eliminate items that are no longer of use.

"A" stands for **ASSIGN, APPLY and ALLOT**:
Assign categories, apply labels, and allot holders.

"N" stands for **NOTE**:
Note which discarded items require special handling, such as hazardous waste.

"S" stands for **SUSTAIN**:
Sustain this new lifestyle by using the methods in this guide.

"E" stands for **ENJOY**:
Enjoy all the new space and time that's now available.

Now let's plunge in for a C.L.E.A.N.S.E. deep dive.

"C" = Concentrate

Concentrate on one area and one room at a time.

Concentrate only on a single room or area until it's done, or else too many distractions beckon. You could be working in the garage, discover a mug and think, "Oh, this belongs in the kitchen," and so that's where you take the mug. There you discover a stapler on the kitchen counter. "Why isn't this in the upstairs office?" and head for the stairs. Once in the office, you find a sweater that belongs in the main bedroom's closet, and off you go.

By the end of the session, you've wandered into every room, but don't see any notable difference anywhere. Concentrating on that one area to create clear progress will tamp down your anxiety and lift up your pride.

MOVING MOMENTS

Just say the word "Palmdale" and my face will lose all expression. Palmdale's positioned in a distant spot in northern Los Angeles County, and a job we had there lives in infamy. A man's sister hired us to help him pack and clear out his home so he could move to the city she lived in. Tom had sent his sister a few photos, which she passed onto us. They showed boxes stacked up in a few rooms. From what I saw, I knew it would be a challenging job, but we'd seen its like before.

"Hah!" said the cosmos to my asinine assumption.

On the back porch, stacks of decrepit bins and boxes reached the roof overhanging it. There was a narrow, ragged trail leading into the house, along with similar ones between the piles of boxes and file cabinets that had taken over the home's interior.

When I saw all this while breathing in a vicious assault of cat pee odor, my knees became soggy and my innards percussive. That Tom was as challenging as the environment he'd created didn't help matters.

But we were entrusted with this job. We had to begin somewhere, and I knew that was up to me. I looked at the overstuffed back porch, which was the de facto entrance to the house. I got his permission to begin there. Each time he told us something on the porch belonged someplace else and to take it there, we'd simply tuck it off to the side or just inside the back door.

He wanted to move us around to other areas of his house, but we continued to concentrate on the task at hand: clearing the back entrance of his home. That would make it a safer place for him to live and also provide us with an area to stage things we had to bring outside the home once we were able to work inside.

As I recall, we got through much of the stuff on the back porch that first day. He could gauge how much had been accomplished, as could we. But that's only because we didn't deviate. If we had, we would have wound up as lost in that quagmire as he was.

For the next session, we moved onto his

> garage. As the door drew up, my stomach dropped to the ground and would have run away if it could. Behind that day lay a taut, three-dimensional puzzle of furniture that came within an inch of the door and half a foot of the ceiling.
>
> But I had my colleagues with me and knew, once again, that they felt just as I did. I had to find a way to continue moving us forward. I summoned the most confident voice I could and said, "Okaayyy… let's start over on the left and work our way across to the right. We can just go layer by layer."
>
> And that's how we began to sort the garage, despite Tom's best efforts to impede our progress.

"L" = Localize:

Localize items where they're actually used.

Locate items where they're put to use. You want to work with your parents' existing systems, not against them. If they pile paid bills and receipts atop the washing machine in the garage as they come and go from their car, then plant the filing cabinet in their garage.

If they take their medication in the kitchen because they need to consume food with it, then find a suitably sized container and organize their medicine in a low kitchen cabinet so they won't have to stretch high to reach it.

> ## MOVING MOMENTS
>
> My company's first client needed our organizing services. We began in her bedroom, where she had two years' worth of bills neatly stacked all along the baseboards around the room because she'd been paying her bills in her bedroom, seated on the edge of her bed with her television on, and then "filing" the paid bills along the edges of her floor.
>
> During our initial consultation, she said, "I guess I should start paying my bills at the desk in the living room." It was really more a question than a statement, and her living room had its own … um … difficulties.
>
> "This is where you pay your bills, right?" I asked, pointing to her bed. She nodded. "Then let's work with the system you already have in place and build out from there. We'll just get a cute filing cabinet and file rack for your bedroom."
>
> During my next visit, we sorted through all the bills along the baseboard and set up the filing cabinet and file rack in her bedroom. Months later, I followed up by phone and inquired about the bedroom bill-paying system. "I love it!" she said. "It's so easy and I can put things away so fast." Mission accomplished.

"E" = Eliminate:

Eliminate items that are no longer of use.

Yes, this may seem obvious, yet so many people do keep many things they'd don't use – and that means eliminating items is always the roaring lion's share of the work. You'll want to separate items into categories such as:

- Keep
- Sell or donate
- Discard

Choose nomenclature that makes sense to your parents. You can also use:

- Yes
- No
- Maybe

With this set of categories, the "Maybe" pile is for items that someone isn't quite ready to let go of during the initial sorting and needs to mull things over. It's frequently the biggest stack of all. Be sure to save some time at the end of the sorting session to review this pile. You'll be surprised by how much of it will ultimately land in the "No" pile. These things just needed a bit more time, a bit more acknowledgement, before your parents could bid farewell.

I once had a client who, during our initial call, said she was a "hoarder"[13] because her husband had said she was. (She wasn't[14].) Laurie was sentimental about her possessions, so we used categories that struck an emotional chord:

- Friends
- Acquaintances
- Strangers

These descriptors worked perfectly for her, because they helped her measure the emotion attached to each of her possessions. "Acquaintances" in this case means the same thing as "Maybe."

Use whichever words your parents like. Or make up your own, and feel free to be as comedic as you'd like. A sense of humor definitely helps ease the way throughout this whole process.

> **SMART MOVE TIP:**
> I've found that the word "discarding" lands more gently than "trashing," "throwing out," or "tossing away," and make it easier to get your parent to place a worn but much-loved item in the bin.

Whatever you call the discard pile, be sure to have plenty of big trash bags at the ready to keep broken parts and their accumulated dust bunnies from taking over the room.

Since we're on the subject of supplies, here's a short list of sorting and downsizing provisions to have on hand:

- The aforementioned trash bags
- Latex gloves for dirtier areas
- Plastic zipper bags of different sizes – gallon, quart, and small (2" x 3" to 3" x 5") – for holding similar, small items securely

If you think you'll encounter sharp objects, have thicker gloves standing by.

"A" = Assign, Apply & Allot:

Assign categories, apply labels, and allot holders and containers.

Assigning categories and storing similar items together will make packing a cinch, and make unpacking and putting them away much faster in the new home.

Let's say you're sorting through a desk and you discover a bunch of paper clips, binder clips, and rubber bands all together in a messy heap with all the pencils, pens, and markers. (Test each of these to make sure they all work. If not, bye-bye.) You could sort the fasteners from the writing utensils now as you sort to make it easier later. Or not. You already know which one I'd choose.

Since these items are small, use the plastic zippered bags to store each group separately. Use a marker (that still writes) to label which bag holds what. Your post-move self will thank you later.

There will also, inevitably, be paperwork to sort through. You'll need a filing system that makes sense for this, one that will make important documents easy to find.

INSIDE SCOOP

I once read about an organizer working with a recently divorced woman. She labeled the divorce file "Good Riddance." What a fantastic idea! Instead of being reminded about her painful divorce, her client felt the relief of being free of a toxic situation.

HOW TO MOVE YOUR PARENTS

For filing systems, applying easy-to-read labels is a must. But first your parents need to decide on a consistent way to name and sort the files. Questions to run by them include:

- Do they want to label their car insurance file as "CAR," "AUTO" or "VEHICLE?"
- Do they want to file their home, car, and life insurance as "INSURANCE: HOME" or "HOME: INSURANCE"?
- When you're organizing things chronologically, do they want the most recent things first or the oldest items in front instead?

The more you can give things a name and provide order that's easily understood, the simpler it will be to find those documents when they're needed.

MOVING MOMENTS

One of our biggest jobs ever was with a client living in a 2-bedroom apartment in Beverly Hills. His home was quite tidy and neat – except for the bedroom that served as his office. Over the course of 30 years, he'd created a cave-like environment filled with papers and files, stacked by themselves, or contained within boxes that lined the walls and closet. It was dark and airless - and he had to carefully guide his tall, 78-year-old frame over stacks of boxes and loose papers to climb into the seat at his desk.

Over the course of two months, we thoroughly sorted and organized all his paperwork. Some of it was barely legible. Some was covered by mold, the result of a broken water pipe in a previous apartment. There were multiple corporations, two bankruptcies, and documents from numerous court cases.

We separated the paperwork into business and personal, and from there assigned the business papers to whichever corporation they belonged to. There were six of them in total, plus his current real estate business. We created a few hundred folders, and I think we wore out a label maker printing out labels for each and every one of them.

He'd bought file cabinets and we assigned categories to each drawer. We allotted holders on his desk to contain his multitude of fasteners, paper clips, and pens.

When we were finished, order and light had returned to the room. He spread his arms wide and said, "This is how an office should be. Now I can grow my business."

"N" = Note:

Note which discarded items require special handling.

Whether it's documents that include Social Security numbers or a box of rat poison, there are plenty of things you'll discover that need special handling. Given the amount of discarded items produced when sorting through an average home, it's vital to properly dispose of sensitive documents and items harmful to our environment.

Documents

If you find shelves of boxes full of old tax returns dating back to 1957 (it totaled 56 years' worth – thanks a lot, Dad), do not toss them in the dumpster or garbage bin. It's entirely legal for anyone to dig through someone else's trash[15]. If they discover that Social Security number, they'll use it for all kinds of nefarious things.

Though you need to keep your returns for a few years (the IRS provides instructions[16]), once that time has passed, shred them!

Also shred (don't toss!) the following:

- Bank and investment statements, no matter how ancient they are
- Old checks and those that will never be used
- Expired credit and debit cards
- Unsolicited or unused credit card offers
- Expired passports, driver's licenses, and government I.D. cards

- Outdated work I.D.s and badges
- Pay stubs
- Medical information
- Tax returns, 1099s, and W-2 forms[17]

All of these documents contain confidential personal information that can be used to steal someone's identity, even if they've passed away.

Don't forget to recycle!

Paper, aluminum, tires, and glass[18] are just a few of the things that can be reused to make new materials and items. In some cases, you can earn some latte money for taking the time to recycle certain items properly.

Toxic trash (AKA household hazardous and electronic waste)

The U.S. Environmental Protection Agency defines hazardous waste as having "properties that make it dangerous or capable of having a harmful effect on human health or the environment,"[19] including "...products that can catch fire, react, or explode under certain circumstances, or that are corrosive..."[20] *Yikes!*

According to the E.P.A., some of the most frequently found are:

- Pesticides
- Herbicides
- Insecticides
- Paints

HOW TO MOVE YOUR PARENTS

- Solvents
- Oil filters
- Light bulbs
- Batteries
- Unemptied aerosol cans
- Ammunition
- Ammonia
- Antifreeze
- Nail polish (Who knew? I didn't until I started my company.)

And there's more! The list is a long one, and you'll find it at the end of this chapter.

It's extraordinary (in a very bad way) how much hazardous waste one domicile can contain, which explains why it's critical to take all of it to an official disposal site[21] to be disposed of as legally and safely as possible.

> ### MOVING MOMENTS
>
> A dear friend and former Clear Home Solutions Project Manager has devoted herself to a deep study of what can be recycled and how, as well as many other things that can improve our ecology and environment.
>
> During our infamous Palmdale job (see details above), we relied on her knowledge

> as we tried to recycle everything we could to avoid adding anything harmful to the local landfill. She became the final arbiter of all discarded items, determining which items could be recycled, which needed to be delivered to an official site for toxins, and which could get a simple heave-ho into the dumpster.
>
> Though we cracked a few jokes about it, her expertise and support in finding ways to recycle things proved to be a great help to us, to our clients, and to our planet.

"S" = Sustain:

Sustain this new lifestyle with these methods.

My intent in creating the C.L.E.A.N.S.E. concept was to teach people how to create order from chaos and then use these methods to maintain that order.

Sustaining an orderly home means tucking everything away immediately after you've finished using it. Don't let things pile up because you don't want clutter and mayhem sneaking back in. If you're considering buying another red sweater, hammer, and/or martini glass set, you might also consider letting the old one go.

More techniques that save time and stress

- *The Two-Minute Rule:* If something will take two minutes or less to do, just do it. Wash that plate you just used. Pay that bill. Put away those paper clips. If you don't, you'll end up with 25 varying, two-minute tasks that, combined, will take an hour or more. When you take care of each task immediately, you'll also get a dose of instant gratification and freedom from that task because it's done. You did it. Game over.[22]

- *P.T.A. – Put That Away:* See above. Once everything has a place it "lives," not only is it easy to find – it's just as easy to put away, and that, of course, makes it easy to find again. So take the time to P.T.A. and that means now, not tomorrow morning, or at some other future time.

- *Map Your Files:* When you create a filing system, especially if it's an extensive one, it's a good idea to make a File Map to show which information is located where and to translate your parents' file-naming system.

- *Ask for Support*: Since you'll be scheduling time for your sessions (remember that Action Plan?), why not ask someone to join you? Even if they just sit there and keep you company, you'll sort and downsize faster and with a lighter heart when someone's cheering you on. You can treat them to lunch, dinner, or a movie afterward.

Whenever you have a session, don't forget to have the music on, with chocolate and some delectable beverages handy. Rather than a task that's dreaded, it will become an event to look forward to.

MOVING MOMENTS

A wonderful woman hired us to help her sister, who'd had Multiple Sclerosis for many years, and whose husband had just been diagnosed with a blood disorder. Things had piled up in many areas. Some closet doors and such needed repair.

Over the course of several Fridays, our team worked diligently to separate the wheat from the chaff, to set up systems that supported her work as a virtual coach, and to get things repaired. She and her husband were a pure delight to work with, and we all went home with goosebumps when our work was complete.

She and I discussed a maintenance program. Given that they both were managing a difficult health condition, it made sense. I checked in with her every couple of months. Each time we spoke, she'd marvel at what we'd all accomplished together. "Everything's still where we set it up!" she said. "I refuse to let this get out of hand again." She recognized the gift her sister had given her and was determined to maintain what our hard work had accomplished.

More than once she told me of the two most important things she'd learned. One was to keep things where she needed and used them ("Localize"). For example,

> anything she needed to support her coaching was kept near the chair she sat in when making her coaching calls.
>
> The other was the Two-Minute Rule. She told me how brilliant it was. I told her I wish I could take credit for it, and that my life, too, had been changed by learning about it.

"E" = Enjoy:

Enjoy all the time you save, and your lightened load.

Need I say more?

> ### INSIDE SCOOP
>
> I grew up as a clutter bug. I knew where everything was, though it may have taken me a while to peel away the layers to find it. I was an "A" student and always met my deadlines, though often just barely.
>
> It wasn't until I'd launched my third business (Clear Home Solutions is my fourth) that I had no choice but to learn about systems. Otherwise, that endeavor would have collapsed under the weight of my disorganization.
>
> So I read, I asked, and I looked around, observing those who were successful at it to see what they did, which tricks and software they used. That's how I learned to keep track of a warehouse full of inventory, down to a single unit. That's how I figured out how to efficiently pack, ship, and unpack my eco-handbags, and then how to move an entire trade show booth to Atlanta one week, New York the next, and then onto Las Vegas the week after that.
>
> That's how I learned about getting things done one bit at a time. Checklists became

> my best pinky-swear friend. QuickBooks, my business, and I became a championship team. My Google Calendar became my color-coded task manager.
>
> I'm living proof that you can learn to be organized. It's simply a matter of understanding the techniques to use.

Household Hazardous & Electronic Waste Items

Be sure to check your local regulations regarding the disposal and handling of hazardous and electronic waste, as well as what constitutes this type of waste in your local jurisdiction. Items may vary, depending on your location.

Electronic Waste

Cell phones	Printers
Computers	Scanners
Electronic games	Stereos
Fax machines	Televisions
Light switches	VCR's and DVD players
Microwaves	

Hazardous Waste[23]

Abrasive cleaners	Asbestos
Air fresheners	Automotive products
Antifreeze	Bug spray

Hazardous Waste[23]

- Car batteries
- Chlorine bleach
- Compact fluorescent light bulbs
- Disinfectants
- Drain cleaners
- Vaping devices / E-cigarettes
- Fertilizers
- Floor, furniture, and shoe polish
- Fluorescent light tubes
- Fungicides, herbicides, and weed killers
- Furniture and paint strippers
- Gasoline and diesel fuel
- Glass/window cleaners
- Hair spray
- Hair relaxers, dyes, and products for permanents
- Household batteries and NiCad batteries
- Insecticide
- Medical needles / sharps waste (may require safe and special containment)
- Medicine (check regulations)
- Mercury thermometers
- Nail polish and nail polish remover
- Oven cleaners
- Pet products (flea collars and sprays)
- Pool chemicals
- Propane tanks (household size)
- Rat, mouse, snail, and slug poisons
- Rug & upholstery cleaners
- Solvents
- Spray paints
- Stains and varnishes

HOW TO MOVE YOUR PARENTS

Transmission and
brake fluid

Thinners and
turpentine

Tub, tile, and toilet
bowl cleaners

Used motor oil and
oil filters

---

13 I learned early on that when someone says they're a "hoarder" they're not. It's just clutter on surfaces like desks, coffee tables, and countertops. A person who does hoard might mention how their "collections" upset the people around them.

14 There was one room and a corner in another with a few heaps of items. Spouses and life partners frequently project onto the other what they're doing. In fact, her husband had squirreled away much more than she had.

15 The 1988 U.S. Supreme Court decision California vs. Greenwood found that there's no expectation of privacy regarding trash that is left for collection in an area that is publicly accessible, such as your street. "California v., Greenwood," Wikipedia, accessed January 29, 2025, https://en.wikipedia.org/wiki/California_v._Greenwood.

16 "How long should I keep records," Internal Revenue Service, accessed January 26, 2025, https://www.irs.gov/businesses/small-businesses-selfemployed/how-long-should-i-keep-records.

17 This list varies across different information resources, but these are the most consistently suggested. Check with an accountant or attorney to see if they recommend additional documents for shredding.

18 "How Do I Recycle Common Recyclables," U.S. Environmental Protection Agency, last updated November 23, 2024, https://www.epa.gov/recycle/how-do-i-recycle-common-recyclables.

19 "Learn the Basics of Hazardous Waste," U.S. Environmental Protection Agency, last updated March 24, 2025, https://www.epa.gov/hw/learnbasics-hazardous-waste.

20 "How Do I Recycle Common Recyclables," U.S. Environmental Protection Agency, last updated November 23, 2024, https://www.epa.gov/recycle/how-do-i-recycle-common-recyclables#hhw.

21 Check your local regulations regarding the proper handling and disposal of hazardous and electronic waste, including what constitutes that waste. This may not be a complete list, depending on your location.

22 This rule was inspired by David Allen's book Getting Things Done: The Art of Stress-Free Productivity. Reading it transformed my life. For real.

23 "Too Toxic to Trash," Department of Water & Power, County of Los Angeles, accessed January 15, 2025, https://dpw.lacounty.gov/epd/hhw/pdf/HHW-EWaste_Products.pdf.

The Obstacle of Memory

If only downsizing were as simple as assigning each possession to one category or another. You already know, or you'll soon discover, how the amount of memories and emotions draped around an object inhibits the ability to let go of it, no matter its state of repair.

The items that people tend to cling to most include kitchen items, tools, photographs, and clothing. I've found the latter is by far the most difficult to sort through, and I think once you learn to capably sort through your parents' clothes, you'll be able to use these methods with everything else.

> ## SMART MOVE TIP:
>
> When frustration can no longer be held at bay and anger makes your eyes throb, please walk outside. Check in with yourself. Your reactions may be just as reactive as those of your parents. Instead, tap into the fear that's driving it. Don't back away from the truth. Go there. Accept that you won't hear your parents' voices or watch emotions enliven their faces forever.

> Talk to your parents about things you've cherished, what you love about them, and family vacations you will never forget. You all have the chance to make this episode of your family's history a transformative experience for all generations. That would make for a very satisfying ending to this story.

The Clothing Quagmire

Our emotions attach themselves to clothing because the fit of the fabric rests on our skin and envelopes our bodies with warmth. Some we don only for special occasions, and so memories lie within each thread. Thinking of clothes and the accessories that accompany them this way reveals why letting go can be so trying.

Time to begin.

We all have clothing we wear regularly, and a good way to ease into this sorting process is to separate these from all their other garments. Since, on average, we only regularly wear 15% to 20% of what resides in our closets and drawers, these shouldn't be hard to pluck from the rest.

But you're counting on what your parent claims rather than visual proof of what they wear on a regular basis. If you have at least six months until Move Day, use the method below to figure out which clothing is actually worn:

- Hang everything in the closet backward, meaning the closed side of the hanger's hook faces the back of the closet while the open part of the hook faces you.
- After a piece of clothing is worn and washed, ask your parent to hang it in the usual way, with the closed end of the hanger's hook facing them.
- When Move Day is on the horizon, scan the closet to see which hooks face which way. You'll clearly see what's been worn in the last half-year, and that should aid the decisions about which items need to move with your parents, and which can remain behind.

If you don't have sufficient time for that, take your parents' word for it. Pull their frequently worn clothes out from the different places they dwell and lay them across the bed. Now that they're gathered in one group, hang them together on the closet rung and in drawers only for them, set apart from the rest.

And then there's formal wear and other outfits worn only for rare and important events, such as weddings. If a piece has been worn in the past three to five years and it still passes all the tests that follow, it can be a keeper.

But if your dad quit playing the bagpipes four years ago and doesn't intend to pick them up again, any kilts can probably go.

> ### SMART MOVE TIP:
>
> As people age, there's another reason they may struggle to let go of apparel: Sometimes they just want something to have a second life, to not let it perish. The more they can envision who'll be wearing it, the more they may be willing to part with it.
>
> Suggest that they offer that seventh pair of Oxfords to someone they know in the hopes that person will accept them. Or remind them that donating those shoes may help someone else who's budget-strapped wear them to a job interview.

Culling Crowded Closets

Now onto all the clothes that linger in the closet and rarely see daylight. Ready? Then let's leap off the high dive together:

- Pull out all the clothes from one part of the closet and heap them on the bed.
- Next, sort "like with like," as in gather all the short-sleeve shirts together on one area of the bed, place all the jeans in another spot, sweaters in another, and so on.
- Choose a group to start with, such as the sweaters. If there are, say, six red sweaters, separate them from the other sweaters.
- Examine each one for holes, tears, and stains. If you

spy any of these, that item doesn't go in the moving van.

- If your mom or dad resists, try using the term "compromised" rather than torn, damaged, or any other word that implies destruction. "Compromised" is a milder term I once read about, and it's very effective.

- If they claim they'll get it repaired, ask them how long it's been lying dormant in their closet. If they say more than a year, or nothing at all, find a gentle way to say that, if they haven't repaired it by now, they never will.

- Here's a loaded question: Does it fit?

- This is the most brutal part of sorting clothes, so steel yourself ahead of time.

- If the answer comes out "yes" but your own eyes say "nope," ask what size they're wearing and compare.

- Next, the proper response to, "I'm going to lose weight so I can wear it again," is, "Yes, you will lose those twenty pounds. But once you do, your body won't have the same proportions it did before. Plus there'll be new fashion trends and colors. Why not celebrate with a shopping spree and let go of these old clothes instead?" (You have my permission to quote me verbatim.)

If multiple red sweaters have passed all these tests, ask your parent to choose no more than two favorites. Tell them once you've gone through everything else and there's still some room on a rung, those other sweaters get a second chance.

> ## SMART MOVE TIP:
>
> I can personally attest to losing the weight and the old clothes still won't fit. During the first five years of running Clear Home Solutions, I was planted at my desk or in the car driving between meetings. Between fast food and lack of exercise, I piled on twenty pounds.
>
> At the age of 57, realizing I needed to set myself up for a healthy later life, I adjusted my ways and shed my "excess baggage." It took time to gain that weight so it took time to lose it, but I eventually did, only to discover any clothing I'd saved from five years and twenty pounds ago pulled or sagged in uncomfortable places.

Other excuses and how to respond to them:

EXCUSE: "I paid a lot of money for that."

RESPONSE: "How many years ago? And it's not worth anything if you're not wearing it. All it's doing is taking up vital closet real estate. Can you get that sweater to pay rent?"

EXCUSE: "It belonged to my favorite aunt…" or *"I wore that when you graduated!"* (And you graduated forty years ago.)

RESPONSE: Hold up that piece of clothing and repeat their reasoning back to them but add a

> vocal question mark at the end – and if you're both in the mood for it, you might add a bit of humorous commentary. "It belonged to your favorite aunt… when Eisenhower was president?"

You can also ask them to look at it in a mirror. This literal and figurative shift in perspective can work wonders.

> EXCUSE: *"But what if…"* "What if there's a leak in the closet ceiling that wrecks both red sweaters?" "What if someone steals them?"

> RESPONSE: "Well, there are other red sweaters out there, and Amazon's always ready to take your order. Or maybe you can wear the blue one? It does match your beautiful eyes."

I've heard all these excuses repeatedly over the years – including from my own mouth while sorting my own clothes.

In all seriousness, remember that each and every *emotional experience matters*. Just because you don't feel the same way or understand your parents' reactions, recognize that denying or negating their feelings will only make things worse. To reject or be judgmental will only deepen that emotion and may even shut them down entirely.

Instead, ask them to tell you the story behind it, and let them live in that moment again without interruption. You never know what family lore you might otherwise never hear. Listen attentively and thank them for telling such a touching memory.

Remind them that they'll always have that memory, that this sweater isn't the actual love or other strong emotion they're feeling. Offer to take a photo of it or even make a video of them telling the story behind it. Knowing that the story will live on can often help them let that item go.

One final note about the rollercoaster of reactions: If your mom or dad begins to rant, cry, or go off in some other way, *do NOT tell them to "calm down."* This insults their dignity – and, seriously, have you <u>ever</u> seen anyone calm down after being told to calm down? Me, neither.

Decision-Making Drains the Brain

With so many decisions to make, you and your parents will most likely be spent after a couple of hours of this. Making decisions gobbles up everyone's energy since our brains devour a disproportionate amount of calories.[24]

Toward the end of each session, remember to mark where you left off. With clothing, hang the sorted pieces together and wrap a piece of tape or ribbon around the rung where your sorting stopped. You don't want the work you've already done to get mixed up with the unsorted clothes. Downsizing's tough enough without having to retread ground you've already covered.

Congratulate your parents for all they've accomplished. If you've argued, do your utmost to let it go. If they keep yanking on that rope, keep redirecting the conversation. "Dad, that watch is amazing. I forgot who gave it to you. Who was it?"

Onto the next

When there are no more shirts to sort or socks to match, heave a sigh of triumph, and – forgive me – now it's onto the shoes, fashion accessories, kitchen items, tools, and every other category in the house. You've learned these key tenets of sorting and downsizing, and tackling all the rest will make more sense to you.

But for now, just listen to your favorite song and go get something delectable to eat.

> ## MOVING MOMENTS
>
> We once had a client who was moving from one senior living community to another and needed to downsize. Unfortunately, Sheila had created a hoarding situation where she was currently living, partly due to her mobility issues, and she staunchly refused to let any of her clothing go.
>
> My colleague went to Sheila's new place and measured the rung in her closet. We then wrapped a piece of colored tape around the rung in her current closet to show where her new closet's rung would end. We needed to show her exactly how much space she'd have there. "It all has to fit within this space," we told her. "There's no more room beyond that."
>
> She fought us about that, until an idea lit my brain. Sheila would be moved into her new home before her current lease concluded, so we had a little grace period to work with. "This place isn't going to fall off the cliff as soon as you move out," I said. "Let's get the essentials moved in over there and then, if you need something else, we can bring it

> over as we're clearing out what you've already agreed to let go of." Miraculously, she accepted that and eventually let go of a lot of apparel. But the clothing that moved with her left not a cat's whisker's worth of room in her new closet for anything else.
>
> (Sheila also allowed us to throw out several expired tubes of Preparation H – though not the unexpired ones. We'd unearthed them from beneath many piles of items around her apartment. Like many people living in disorganized homes, she kept buying more because she couldn't locate any when she needed it.)

---

24 "While the brain represents just 2% of a person's total body weight, it accounts for 20% of the body's energy use…That means during a typical day, a person uses 320 calories just to think." Markham Heid, "Does Thinking Burn Calories? Here's What the Science Says," Time.com, Time Magazine, September 19, 2013, https://time.com/5400025/does-thinking-burn-calories/.

Undiscovered Treasures in Unexpected Places

The objects in a home tell us stories about those who've dwelt there. The colors, the origins, what they express — each object reveals a sentence or paragraph of the occupant's history. The story may be incomplete, but these possessions color in several pages.

Preparing to leave a home becomes a treasure hunt. Some of the things are known to the family but may have been lost somewhere within the walls. Others have been forgotten and emerge as new discoveries all these years later.

The logbooks my father kept as a World War II pilot were my find. I knew the stories of his Navy days from dozens of tellings throughout my lifetime, but I'd never seen these logbooks. He'd never mentioned them, so I'm sure he thought they'd been lost.

They'd lain at the back of the bottom drawer of a tall filing cabinet, disheveled, with pages all akimbo. I couldn't translate the numbers and letters he'd recorded in them. I only recognized that the scrawled numbers and letters came from a pencil he'd held. (He always had appalling handwriting.) Seeing this, witnessing it, brought dimension to the black-and-white photographs of him sitting in planes, flying them, and grinning into the camera as he knelt on a wing while a buddy took his picture. Probably Gus, who's long passed, too.

These logbooks brought more dimension to these photographs, and to the crazy tales I remember. I'm lucky to have been born, given some of the reckless risks he took. But that's who he was.

Treasure Hunt or Archaeological Dig?

You'll likely unveil your own familial surprises during this journey with your parents. Most of these surprises are delightful, like Dad's logbooks. Others may be damaging, such as love letters from a clandestine affair.

A hoarding situation is less akin to a treasure hunt than to an archaeological dig. Treasures are in there, but the hills and mounds require a lot of time and patience to pull apart, and you get filthy along the way.

There's no predicting what's in that furrowed bundle at the back of the coat closet, or in a box frosted with dust in the attic. These aren't the only places where things long forgotten can settle in.

Garages

I love a good garage. Here, beside old paint cans lining the shelves and beneath the overhead light speckled with dust and spider's webs, undiscovered things may rest.

Garages have often become a storage unit attached to the house, and are likely to contain things like:

- A torn camping tent stashed in the rafters.
- Tile remnants left over from a bathroom floor repair after the plumber cracked those tiles while fixing the toilet.

- Old scraps of carpet.
- Boxes and bags bulging with mysterious and unknown contents.

Neat, organized garages are as rare as six-toed cats or single-horned goats. The chances that two cars will fit in a two-car garage might be fifty-fifty. Often no vehicle fits at all.

This is why garages take so long to work through. Don't try to sort everything all on a single Saturday, because your back, shoulders, and knees will whine about it for days. You'll want an able-bodied buddy or two along to keep you company, help you lift the heavy things, and place donations in your car.

Important supplies and practices

In addition to your regular organizing supplies (listed in the *C.L.E.A.N.S.E. Concept* chapter), garages also call for:

- Thick gloves are de rigueur to shield you from pointy things like errant screws and nails, along with spiders and other creatures who like to nest undisturbed in the dark and quiet.
- Plenty of rags and wipes to clean up that can of motor oil you just tipped over.
- If paint cans containing every color on every wall inside (plus all the colors underneath) won't be put to use, they can join your collection of hazardous waste that you'll dispose of respectfully.

Time-saving tips

Supply cabinets occasionally start out orderly. But that dissolves as the years go by – as labels peel off, things get shoved into back corners, and cans of green beans expire. As for those curious boxes and bags, count yourself lucky if someone labeled any – but only if those labels genuinely describe their contents.

Lean a few new boxes flat against the wall. Should you find breakables inside a tired bag or crumpling box that your parents would like to keep, place them in the new boxes and slide a rag in between each to cushion them.

Any furniture that's sat in a garage for more than one season will have accumulated dust, insects that gnaw, and odors that insult your sense of smell. Maybe that chair or end table is for *someday*. *Someday* you'll have room for it. *Someday* your child will want it. What if *someday* something breaks and you need a replacement?

Someday is as elusive as a dream caught between waking and sleeping, so push that furniture out of the garage and send it elsewhere. Its long rest in the garage has compromised it.

If your parents or a sibling balks, ask:

- "When was the last time you sat in it?"
- "Do I spy a tear in the seat?"
- "If your house burned down tomorrow, would you take the time to find a replacement – and spend the money to purchase it?"

Silence will often be their answer.

How to handle "I want you to have this."

No one knows how to lean on your buttons like your immediate family members.

"You have to take" the china set that's been in the family for three generations, or the turquoise-colored shawl your father's mother wore to every religious service. "That buffet must be very valuable because it's an antique," they'll say, even though three knobs are missing, and a couple of cats used one side as a scratching board decades ago.

The power of that knowing tug on your heartstrings could drag a carrier out to sea.

Yet I'm *not* going to say, "Don't accept them," even though you don't have room, or don't care to make room, for all the things they want to bestow on you.

For the sake of family unity and love, *just say "yes."* Why? Because once that item is in your possession, it now belongs to *you*, so *you* may do with it whatever *you'd* like. You are by no means required to keep it in your home after it's been given to you.

You're allowed to offer it to others dear to you and, if they want it, touchdown! They can pick it up from you. You can also choose to donate it or discard it.

Yet you dread that moment when your parent, with a glowing smile on their face, asks what you did with that buffet they gave you. First, thank them for giving it to you, even though it isn't where they expected it would be.

The rest of your reply depends on how honest your relationship is with them, and how you think the truth may land. If you feel confident with undiluted honesty, you can soften the blow by saying that, as much as you loved and appreciated their gift, you knew someone else who would love it even more, and use it more frequently than you would.

HOW TO MOVE YOUR PARENTS

Even if you donated it, you're still truthful when you say it's in the hands of someone who cherishes it as much as your parent had.

If a harsh tone or tears begin to simmer, politely say it was such a beautiful gift, how much you appreciate their generosity - then redirect the conversation as gracefully as you can.

Sometimes, though, I think a "fiblet" under these circumstances is just fine if it quelches family tumult. You could simply say you're having it refinished, or that it's in storage until you can discern the perfect pride of place for it – and onto the next topic.

Photographs

Your Family's History, Illustrated.

For older adults, photographs are the pictorial memorials of their youth. Not so long ago, photographs were an indulgence, reserved only for the most important of occasions.

It took effort to handle the raw film carefully, to wait to get the photos developed - and then nervously inspect them to see whether each was in focus, properly lit, with the composition just right. These images came in different forms: negatives, slides, and printed photos large and small.

Your parents may want to save all of them. However, a family's collection of photos, in all their various forms, demands a vast amount of storage space in closets, drawers, and attics. Plus, over time, they can fade and deteriorate.

INSIDE SCOOP

I remember watching a pipe burst in our basement when I was very young. My mother hollered, "Our treasures!" as she bolted away from the ruined pipe to rescue boxes of photos, her children's school artwork, and the Valentine's cards we crafted clumsily from construction paper and glue.

These were her pearls and the riches of her heart. That was my mother.

Fortunately, our age of technology offers a brilliant solution: Digitizing. But digitizing and scanning the entire, unsorted collection wastes time and money. You'll wind up preserving a plethora of useless pictures that might include:

- A blurry person in the foreground with perfectly focused trees in the background.
- Well-framed trash bins in the center and smiling friends far off to the side.
- A faultless photo of a very happy couple - whose identities are unknown to all.

Photo collections are vast and innumerable, so downsizing them to the most meaningful pictures require a substantial amount of time. Since you and your family have the move's immediate tasks pressing on you, this project may need to wait until after the move.

Whenever you're all rested and ready to digitize the family photos, you can either:

- Hire a company to organize and scan your physical photos, slides, and negatives.
- Take on the mission yourselves, so long as you or another family member have the time, dedication, and patience to do so.

However you choose to do this, here is a straightforward method to organize those visual gems.

Printed Photos, Slides and Negatives

First, some guidelines for keeping your photos clean and unmarred, your slides and negatives in particular:

- Keep photos away from liquid, mist, or dampness.

- o All beverages should be at least four feet away from any photos. We all know from experience how fast spilled Diet Coke can travel.
- Never store newspapers with your photos. You don't want your photos decorated with newsprint ink.
- Direct sunlight will fade your photos quicker than you think, so keep them well away from it.
- Wearing white cotton, photo-safe gloves while you sort and organize these items prevents oils from hands and fingertips from sullying your images.
- Commandeer the dining room table or a couple of folding tables and set the entire assortment of images there. This will be your Photo Command Center.

The "ABC" Method of sorting photos

I use a widely known sorting system called the "ABC" method because it's clear and uncomplicated. Each letter represents each photo's level of importance and beauty:

- "A" Photos: These are your family's favorite and most impactful photos. They illustrate memorable moments through vibrant images and composition, plus they're in great condition. Think of these as the photos that will reside in frames all around the home or in your family's favorite photo albums.
- "B" Photos: While these aren't as beloved or important as your "A" photos, they do contribute to an important story in your family's history. Though they probably won't go on display, you may want to digitally scan them for posterity.
- "C" Photos: These will soon be sitting by the curb, awaiting the trash truck. They're blurry, faded, or damaged beyond repair. You recognize no one in the photo and there's no information written on the back indicating who it might be. Duplicate photos serve

HOW TO MOVE YOUR PARENTS

no purpose beyond taking up extra space. If someone says they'll send them to relatives, kindly inform them it's better to scan them and share digitally. None of these photos evoke any emotion or recognition, so there's no reason to let them take up space.

Have boxes labeled and ready for each category's photos so you can sort them into the appropriate container.[25] At the end of each session, put the "C" photos in your trash bin.

> **SMART MOVE TIP:**
>
> Blemishes, dust, and discoloration can be removed from photos, and it's an artform all to itself. The best-known software for healing photos in this way is Adobe's Photoshop. But beware: if you detest learning new software, you may want to outsource this to a professional photo restorer.

Sorting all your images will take a lot of time. You have your Photo Command Center at the ready, so schedule some times to do it. Be kind to your eyes by setting a time limit.

As you're going through them all, talk with your parents and family about how to organize them when the sorting's completed. You could organize them using any of these ways:

- Chronologically by decade.
- Chronologically by decade and "A" or "B" category.

- By milestone events (weddings, graduations, births, and marriages) and then by decade.
- Family, decade, and "A" or "B" category.
- Family, milestone events, and decade.

You can make this as granular and complex as you want. But sort using one factor at a time to prevent confusion. Whichever way you choose document following:

- Categories and any subcategories
- How they're labeled
- Any other specific information you think future generations may need to embrace your family's visual history.

This is for prosperity and the legacy of those you love. Try to remember that when it's midnight and a negative just rudely nicked a finger for the fourth time that evening.

Organizing Digital Photos

Use the same technique and sorting system as above but organize them in digital folders rather than using physical boxes and labels.

The main difference is how you label the folders, and whether you choose to devote extra time to adding a filename to each photo. If you do, be very consistent. Document the system you're using and save a record of that system with the scanned photos.

HOW TO MOVE YOUR PARENTS

Using the organizing examples above, you might name your files in these ways (I've included a chart of these examples at the end of the chapter):

- Chronologically by decade

    - [Decade]_ [Assigned Number]
    - 1970_1 (i.e., First photo scanned and saved for this decade)
    - 1980_15 (Fifteenth photo scanned)
    - 2020_134 (134th photo scanned)

- Chronologically by decade and "A" or "B" category

    - [Letter]_[Decade]_ [Assigned Number]
    - A_1970_1
    - B_1980_15
    - A_2020_134

- Milestone events - weddings, graduations, births, and important holidays - and then by decade

    - [Event]_[Decade]_[Assigned Number]
    - Birth_1970_1
    - July 4_1980_15
    - Wedding_2020_134

- Family, decade and "A" or "B" category

    - [Family Surname]_[Letter]_[Decade]_[Assigned Number]
    - Arden_A_1970_1
    - Ortega_B_1980_15
    - Nguyen_A_2020_134

- Family, location, and decade.

- [FamilySurname]_[Location]_[Decade]_[Assigned Number]
- Arden_New York_1970_1
- Ortega_OgdenUT_1980_15
- Nguyen_Toronto_2020_134

Store your digital photos in two places – a cloud storage account and an external drive or flash drive. You'll want a backup in case the online account is hacked, or the drive goes missing.

Photo by photo, decade by decade. Slowly but surely, you'll get it done.

---

25 You might include a "Maybe" category to temporarily hold photos that, at first look, might be a "B" instead of a "C."

How to Name Digital Photo Files

As you organize your digitized photos, there are a variety of ways to name each of these photos in your online folder, if you choose to do so. Be sure to be consistent because you're saving these for posterity. Create a legend or key so that those who may search through these files will be able to understand how you named them.

Organizing method	How to Name Each File (with an example)
Chronologically by decade	[Decade]_[Assigned Number]
	1970_1 (i.e., First photo scanned and saved for this decade)
	1980_15 (Fifteenth photo scanned)
	2020_134 (134th photo scanned)
Chronologically by decade and "A" or "B" category	[Letter]_[Decade]_[Assigned Number]
	A_1970_1

		B_1980_15
		A_2020_134
Milestone events - weddings, graduations, births, and important holidays - and then by decade		[Event]_[Decade]_[Assigned Number]
		Birth_1970_1
		July 4_1980_15
		Wedding_2020_134
Family, decade and "A" or "B" category		Jones_A_1970_1
		Nguyen_A_2020_134
		Ortega_B_1980_15

Family, location, and decade	[Family Surname]_[Location]_[Decade]_[Assigned Number]			
	Jones_New York_1970_1			
	Ortega_Ogden-UT_1980_15			
	Nguyen_Toronto_2020_134			
Individual, year, and "A" or "B" category	[First Name]_[Last Name]_[Decade]_A			
	Samantha Jones_1997_B			
	Lily Nguyen_2003_A			
	Arturo Ortega_2015_B			

Photo Sorting Supplies

Printed Photos, Slides, and Negatives	Why?
White, photo-safe cotton gloves	Keep the oils from your fingers and hands off them.
Clean (new, ideally)	Categorizing and saving your photos.
Post-It Notes	Use while doing initial sorting.
Index Cards	Use while doing initial sorting.
Pen and/or Pencil	Use while doing initial sorting.
Notebook	Keep track of any abbreviations you use and/or anything else worth noting.
Label maker / Masking Tape & Marker	Labeling the boxes of photos.

Family, location, and decade	[Family Surname]_[Location]_[Decade]_[Assigned Number]
	Jones_New York_1970_1
	Ortega_Ogden-UT_1980_15
	Nguyen_Toronto_2020_134
Individual, year, and "A" or "B" category	[First Name]_[Last Name]_[Decade]_A
	Samantha Jones_1997_B
	Lily Nguyen_2003_A
	Arturo Ortega_2015_B

Photo Sorting Supplies

Printed Photos, Slides, and Negatives	Why?
White, photo-safe cotton gloves	Keep the oils from your fingers and hands off them.
Clean (new, ideally)	Categorizing and saving your photos.
Post-It Notes	Use while doing initial sorting.
Index Cards	Use while doing initial sorting.
Pen and/or Pencil	Use while doing initial sorting.
Notebook	Keep track of any abbreviations you use and/or anything else worth noting.
Label maker / Masking Tape & Marker	Labeling the boxes of photos.

Digital and/or Scanned Photo Items	
Online storage account	Keep your photos out in the cloud so you can easily share them, and, if they're lost or destroyed, easy access for you.
External hard drive or flash drive with sufficient storage to save all your scanned items.	Always have a back up!

Vital Documents & How to Find Them

Photos are the picture book of your family's legacy, but your parents' estate plan, healthcare directive, and financial documents are the ledgers and instructions that *secure* their legacy. During this transition, someone besides your parents needs to know where these vital records.

If their attorney has them, good. But what's the attorney's name, location, and phone number, and who has that information? At least one other person needs to know.

Why be concerned with this while you tussle in the thickets of move preparations? Because we all know, but don't want to think, that life is delicate, and death can step through the doorway at any time. One of my dearest friends lost her father as he and her mother were packing up to move to a senior living community in another state. A major stroke cruelly took him all of a sudden, without a warning shot across the bow.

Perhaps you understand this by now. But do your parents?

In our culture, we treat discussions about death and its finality as morbid and forbidden. Yet we all need to have (and normalize) these conversations with our family members. Doing so can be a loving relief for both generations.

HOW TO MOVE YOUR PARENTS

If you haven't had this conversation yet, you need to. And this includes discussing their will, healthcare directive, and financial situation. I remain deeply grateful to my late my 90-year-old father for having had all of his documentation in place when he passed. Every "i" dotted, every "t" crossed.[26] Then again, that was my father.

> ### MOVING MOMENTS
>
> A friend of mine - an excellent Registered Nurse and care manager - worked with a very successful doctor who'd recently had his attorney updated his estate plan. The doctor had been married twice and had two sets of offspring, some of whom weren't included in his earlier will.
>
> The doctor, a cardiologist in his mid-80s, had those documents in his desk when he died from a heart attack. When a family member pulled his estate plan from the drawer, they discovered <u>he had never signed it.</u>
>
> The family suffered for a few years in probate court before it was all settled – and all for the want of a signature.

These papers reveal your parents' wishes when they're no longer there to speak for themselves. This is how they can control what happens to them, and to their assets, even after they've departed. If dementia invades, they'll have more control of their future and their destiny, even as their mind fades, because they documented their wishes.

While I've mentioned the most essential documents, there's more that needs to be known. Who'll take care of their pets if they can no longer care for them? Who gets that ruby brooch or those diamond cufflinks?

It's not enough to mention something to your spouse, to a child, to a friend, or to your doctor. You must, in this litigious age, have all that information fully and legally documented, signed, and in a known location.

I can't count all the times adult children have tasked my team with locating a will, a trust, or a deed because they're sure "It's in there somewhere!" Besides the many documents we've located over the years, we've also unearthed some unexpected items:

- A pearl necklace inside a folder in a file cabinet
- A skull in a box
- $50,000 in a bag of old bras…
- …accompanied by another $10,000 in a pair of dirty socks

Nothing shocks me anymore.

Another assignment we frequently get from clients is locating keys. Do you know where your parents keep their safe deposit box key? How about the deed to the house and the car's title? The key to the storage unit, the key for the outdoor shed, and the combination to the safe at the back of the main bedroom's closet – where are they?

HOW TO MOVE YOUR PARENTS

I've witnessed how crushing it is to not know these details - the scrambling, the quarreling, and the cruel dread of not knowing - all while in the claws of enormous grief. I can also attest to the relief and clarity that comes with having sound estate planning documents, and knowing where to find them. Dad had a sound plan and had shown me where to find it. My sisters and I were lucky.

What about your own children, your own heirs? You need to have this discussion with them, too. And if you haven't put together your estate plan, it's high time you did.

No one knows the future, but we can all make a plan for our years to come.

---

[26] In case you're wondering why I don't mention my amazing mother here, she was taken by cancer when she was only 58 years old and I was 26. Dad handled everything after she passed. I only had to handle my grief, deep though it was.

Vital Documents & Keys

This lists many important documents, including parts of a comprehensive estate plan. Be sure to consult with an attorney who specializes in estate planning as every situation, like every family, is unique. Also, feel free to add documents to this list if you want to make sure others know where they are, and that they exist.

	Document Name	Location
☐	**Estate Plan Documents**	
☐	Will	
☐	Living Trust Documents	
☐	Durable Power of Attorney	
☐	Durable Financial Power of Attorney	

	Document Name	Location
☐	Health Care Proxy	
	Health Care Directive/Living Will	
☐	**List of Asset Accounts**	
☐	Bank Accounts	
☐	Credit Card Accounts	
☐	Investment Accounts	
☐	**List of Insurance Policies & Policy Numbers**	

	Document Name	Location
☐	Homeowners Insurance Policy	
☐	Car Insurance Policy	
☐	Life Insurance Policy	
☐	Long-Term Care Insurance Policy	
☐	**Real Estate Documents**	
☐	Deed(s) of Trust	
☐	List of Other Property Owned (if applicable)	

	Document Name	Location
☐	**Contact List**	
☐	Key Family Member, Friend, or Contact (who will notify others)	
☐	Doctors	
☐	Neighbors	
☐	Attorney(s)	
☐	Caregivers or Home Care Agency	
☐	Accountant	

	Document Name	Location
☐	Insurance Broker(s)	
☐	Other Emergency Contacts	
☐	**If There are Pets**	
☐	Veterinarian	
☐	Online Log-In Information & Websites	
☐	**Other**	
☐	Car Title(s)	

	Document Name	Location
☐	Combinations to any Safes or Locked Compartments	
☐	Burial Plans / Funeral Arrangements	
☐	**Keys**	
☐	Car Keys	
☐	Safe Deposit Box Key	
☐	Home/Property Keys	
☐		

How to Pack & Label Like a Pro

<u>Heads up</u>: This section has an ocean of information, so you may want to read it through a couple of times to absorb it.

Chances are you'll begin some of the packing during the sorting and downsizing process. Excellent! Getting a head start on packing things that are rarely used is time well spent, and you can stash those boxes in the garage, any infrequently used area, and in the back corner of a room.

Supplies

Packing requires more than just boxes and tape. (See the detailed packing supply list at the end of this chapter.) Make sure you gather these supplies ahead of time, so you're not scrambling when you're in a good packing rhythm.

> ### INSIDE SCOOP
>
> Rhythm happens! I miss packing dishware. I found the simple motion and repetition of packing plates, bowls, and mugs, one after the other to be soothing, almost meditative. This is not my only eccentricity. I can also look at a wall and know exactly where to hang a photo or piece of art. It's my silly superpower.

You can lessen your supply costs by looking for lightly used boxes. Here's how:

- Reuse sturdy delivery boxes so long as they're free of rips, holes, and any sagging.
- Visit your local grocery and liquor stores because they often have empty leftover boxes from shipments they just received.
- Request moving boxes on Next Door, BuyNothing, OfferUp, and on your social media pages.
- Keep your eyes open when driving because you may pass a home with a moving truck being unloaded. Ask if you can take away some or all of their used boxes, bubble wrap, and packing paper for free.

To reiterate: *Any used boxes or other packing materials you use must be in good shape or they won't do the job.* It's fine if the packing paper is wrinkled or the used bubble wrap is torn in a couple of places.

Additional Safety Precautions

I know you've been following all the safety measures for downsizing, right?

There are a few more to add as you pack, and you must make sure everyone follows them, including any professionals you've hired.

If they or anyone else claims these measures are unnecessary, rest assured I have twelve years of reasons for them. Keeping everyone safe and sound has always been a top priority.

Countertops and Tables, Yes – Stovetops NOOOOO!!!

When table-top and counter space in the kitchen is limited, a quiet stovetop may seem like a good place to set down a box on top of the dormant burners.

STOP THAT THOUGHT RIGHT THERE.

It's imperative that no one packs boxes or places anything else on top of the stove. Someone could walk by and bump a burner knob, leading to a fire that endangers everyone in your parents' home, and possibly their neighbors.

Tipping is Good for the Movers – But Not Your Furniture

To keep bookcases, file cabinets, and tall dressers from tipping over onto you, pack them from the top down so you keep the weight at the bottom to anchor them.

Just Because it's a Large Box Doesn't Mean You Can Pack a Horse in It

No matter how large a cardboard box may be, it's still just cardboard and packing tape holding its bottom together. Yes, you can pack larger, bulkier items in them, but they need to be on the lighter side or you'll break the poor box's bottom. Nothing and no one wants a broken bottom.

Speaking of Which…

Backs as well as boxes can only support so much weight. Asking for another set of biceps, abs, and thigh muscles can prevent herniated discs and other body damage. Be sure to offer your own assistance when you see someone else struggling.

The Basic Rules of Packing

Personal and Necessary Items

Set aside the following for you or your parent to *hand carry on Move Day*:

- Important keys – and make sure you don't pack the house or car keys inside a furniture drawer!
- Medications
- Valuable jewelry
- Phone charger

Your jewelry will be safe, and you'll likely need the other items at some point.

Pack an "Open First" carton that contains bed linens, toilet paper, toothbrushes, soap, and paper towels. Have the movers load this box into the truck *last* so it will come out *first*.

4 Reasons You Want to Make a Packing List

Allow me to sing the praises of the almighty Packing List! While it will require additional time and may *seem* like an annoyance, your Packing List will ultimately offer you these key advantages:

1. You'll be much more organized during this packing stage. Your toiletries, for example, won't end up in a box alongside the laundry detergent because they belong in different rooms.

2. You'll also know which box the toiletries and laundry detergent are actually in, because you've recorded that on

your Packing List.

3. When everything's being moved into your parents' new home, you can stand at the door with the Packing List and check off each box as it goes past the door jamb.

4. If one box or more doesn't come through that new front door, you'll be able to tell the moving company exactly what you're looking for, and they can't claim that the box never existed.

Information to record in your Packing List:

- The room or area from which the box's items came.
- The room or area that box is destined for in the new home.
- A one- to five-word description of the contents of the box. "Dishes" or "Knick-Knacks" will do.
- That box's assigned number.

Assigning numbers to each box can be tricky when you have multiple people packing. If, heaven forbid, it's just you, you can add the numbers to each box as you pack them.

More likely you'll have others packing with you at times. Provide each packer with a notepad for jotting down these details for each box they pack – except for the box's number. At the end of the session, collect these notes, and you'll be the one to assign a number to each box as you add it to your Packing List.

General Packing Tips

All these are part of our Clear Home Solutions' training:

- Use heavy-duty packing tape.

- Place a cushion of paper below and on top of a box's contents so that the packed contents are safe from the box cutting blade when they're opened.

- Add heavier items to the bottom of each box for stable lifting. (You'd think this would be obvious, but I've learned that it isn't.)

- Keep the weight evenly distributed on both sides of the box, so it won't roll over inside the truck or anywhere else.

- When you come across an item to pack that's damaged or has a missing part, place a piece of tape[27] on the damaged area, take a photo of it, and after you've wrapped it, write "DAMAGED" on the packing paper surrounding it.

- Take a photo of the damage, because sometimes items acquire more damage in transit, and your photo will help you prove that.

- When you're ready to seal the box closed, carefully lean across the top of it before you grab your tape gun. If the top becomes concave to any degree, you need to add paper to the top. Ensure that box feels solid before you seal it shut so that if a heavy box is placed on top of it in the moving truck, it won't cave in and damage the items inside.

As vital as these basic rules and procedures are, it's just as important to understand how to keep everything intact.

Fragile Items

- Place fragile items in a box vertically, whenever possible.
- You don't necessarily need bubble wrap. Several

sheets of packing paper used together will create a lot of cushioning around something that's delicate. Also, if you face triple-degree heat on move day, the bubble wrap's plastic can melt and adhere to what it's supposed to be protecting.

- Tissue paper or even toilet paper is great for weaving through the fingers of delicate statuary and sculpture, as well as the thin handles of cherished teacup sets.
- It's far better to over-protect than under-protect.

Electronic Items

- Using masking tape and a marker, label the cord and plug for each electronic item to indicate which one it belongs to, and where it plugs in.
- Take a photo, too, in case the label falls off in transit.
- Label each remote to indicate which device it controls. Pack them carefully and together. If there's room, you can add them to your "Open First" box. Otherwise, set aside a specific box just for your remotes.
- Pack older, bulkier monitors screen-side down because their bases are fragile. Add a substantial amount of paper cushioning beneath them.
- When packing computers, make sure any disk drives are free of CDs and DVDs.
- For printers and other electronics that use ink and toner, remove the ink and toner cartridges for any long-distance move.
- Make sure to "lock" any scanners prior to moving. Their instruction manuals will show you how.
- Record turntables should be packed flat.

Kitchen Items

- Pack the dishware first. Label one carton "Kitchen - Immediate Needs" so it can be opened first among the kitchen boxes.
- Check ovens and microwaves for pots and pans. It's easy for those to be overlooked.
- When packing pots and pans, nest them together with occasional paper added to muffle any banging noises.
- Pack metal lids with their affiliated pot or pan. Wrap glass lids and pack them separately.
- Empty toasters and toaster ovens and remove any crumbs so things won't get messy.
- With microwaves, wrap the inside plate, then place it back inside the microwave. Pack paper or a towel around it to keep it in place.
- Pack knife sets in their knife block whenever possible.
- With loose knives, make a cardboard sheath using a box flap, or wrap a thick layer of paper around sheathed knife. Then label it "Sharp Knife."
- Always pack cleaning supplies and other liquids that might leak, such as wine and liquor, upright and in a box you've lined with a plastic garbage bag.
- For salt and pepper shakers, place the end with holes inside a small plastic bag and tape the bag around it so that anything that escapes will fall into the plastic bag. Then wrap the item.
- Pack glassware vertically, placing each one's "cup" on the bottom. Wrap those stems carefully!
- Packing supply stores, online and off, offer "dish packs" and "glass packs" kits. These kits are built for

dishware sets and glassware sets, and usually come with dividers and foam pouches to assist you in packing. (We usually use regular boxes for our clients, but using these kits may save you time.)

Bookcases

- Assign a letter (A, B, C, etc.) to each bookcase.
- Assign a number (1, 2, 3, etc.) to each bookshelf. Because you'll want to unpack the books from the bottom up, the #1 bookshelf should be the bottom bookshelf.
- Pack one shelf per carton and label that carton. For example, box "A-1" would indicate those books that belong on the bottom shelf of bookcase A. If you need more than one carton per shelf, then you would add "1 of 2," "2 of 2" etc. to the labeling.
- If individual bookshelves in a bookcase are held in place by dowels, be sure to keep track of those dowels by placing them in a small plastic bag and, using painter's tape, attaching them to their respective bookcase. Also keep track of the height measurements between each bookshelf in each bookcase.

Books and Vinyl Records

- Before packing a book, fan through all of its pages. I've watched dollars, checks, and drivers' licenses spill from them.
- When packing books, make sure to create a layer of paper padding at the bottom, just as you would if

packing any other box.

- Pack hardcover books as they appear on the bookshelf: have the spines perpendicular to the bottom of the box and then line them up accordingly.
- Pull all vinyl records from their sleeves to make sure they are A) intact and B) to see if there's anything else inside the sleeve. Place the record back in the sleeve to pack it.
- Pack these vinyl records vertically, not flat or stacked on one top of one another.

Clothing: So Hard to Sort, but so Easy to Pack

- Check all pockets in each piece of clothing and anything else that has pocketry. Cash, jewelry, and nasty things frequently tumble out.
- Use "wardrobe boxes" for all the items hanging in your closets.[28] These come with a rung, so just pull the clothing on hangers from your closet and then simply hang them on the box's rung. It makes it so easy to unpack in your new home, especially because you can keep your clothing's organization intact.
- Add blankets and pillows to the bottom of the box. Their weight will stabilize the box and its contents.
- Pack loose or folded clothing in a box, and over-pack the box as it will likely need to support the weight of another box on top of it in the moving truck.
- Pack your shoes in a box. For your more elegant and valuable pairs, wrap each shoe in a layer of tissue paper to prevent accidental scuffs.

Linens and Towels

- Use linens, towels, and dish rags as cushioning in boxes to save on packing paper.
- Pack the remaining ones together in their own box or on the bottom of a wardrobe box.

Weapons, Ammunition, Explosives, Oxygen Tanks & Other Combustibles – Including Oxygen Tanks

- Discuss these ahead of time with your moving company because most companies won't allow these on their moving trucks for liability reasons.
- You'll need to hire a company that specializes in safely and legally transporting these dangerous materials.
- If you choose to transport your weapons and ammunition yourself, become an expert about the regulations covering these in each state you're moving from, moving to, and any state you'll travel through with them.
    - As you may already know, regulations can vary widely from state to state. Risking arrest in the middle of your move is something that will make it that much memorable – in a horrible way.

If, even with these instructions, you don't feel comfortable packing certain things, like fragile objects, you can have professionals pack those items while you handle the rest. This isn't an all-or-nothing situation.

> **SMART MOVE TIP:**
> I've based this packing timeframe on having at least a two-month lead up to Move Day for a three-ish bedroom home. If you have less time, adjust accordingly.

Local Moves vs. Long-Distance Moves

Local moves are usually defined as being within 400 miles or less from the origin point. Beyond that, it's considered a long-distance move. Ask each moving company you interview about how they would categorize your move.

Local Moves

- You can save time with a short move by leaving the contents inside drawers just where they are – but only those that are unbreakable!
- Add paper cushioning to these items so they won't roll around or fall out while they're in transit.

Long-Distance Moves

- It's vital to create a detailed packing list to be sure all boxes and items arrive at the new home.
- Do not leave any items in furniture cabinets or the drawers of dressers, desks, nightstands, etc.
- Pack these drawer items starting from the top drawer to the bottom drawer, using the same system as bookcases and bookshelves (see above).
- When packing more than a single drawer's contents

in one box, separate each drawer's contents by placing a layer of paper atop the items from one drawer and writing which drawer they came from (1, 2, 3, etc.). Then pack the next drawer's contents above that paper. After that, use another sheet to identify where the top contents came from.

- When labeling these boxes, indicate which piece of furniture the contents came from, and which drawer.

International Moves...

...are a beast unto themselves. All your possessions will require a bill of lading and will have to pass through customs. You'll need to hire a Customs Broker (sometimes known as a Customs House Brokerage) to assist you since regulations, tariffs, and bureaucracy differ with each country – along with languages and alphabets. These are moves that require extensive planning and lead time, so it's best to begin the process at least a year ahead.

How to Label your Moving Boxes

<u>Do not skip this step</u>.

It's the difference between your movers taking two or three hours to carry items into your new home versus spending eight hours or more opening every box to figure out where each box needs to go.

What to know when unpacking and organizing your new home as smoothly and efficiently as possible:

- The room or area each box is assigned to in the new home.
- A brief description of the items inside ("Books,"

"Dishware," "Mom's Clothes").

- Whether the items within are fragile or not.
- The number assigned to the box.

Because of all these details, how you label the boxes is as important as how they're packed. So here's your box-labeling crash course:

- After you've sealed the box, grab a thick black marker to do the labeling.
- Use that marker to write down the box's number in the upper right corner of one side of the box, then circle that number.
- In the center, using large letters, add the name of the room or area where the box belongs in the new home.
- An inch or so below that, use your regular marker to record the box's contents.
- If any of the items packed in the box are fragile, place a "fragile" sticker on the upper left corner of the top of the box AND wrap "fragile" stickers around the two opposing sides of the box.
    - This way, no matter which way the box is turned, everyone sees that the contents are fragile.[29]
- If you're packing a box that was previously used and has markings on it, use the marker and neatly black out the other markings on the box.
- Write "DO NOT UNPACK" on boxes that contain unsorted items, such as paperwork. (Remember to plan a time to organize them after the move!)

Timeline for Packing

I saved this for the end of this section so you'd already understand the mechanics of packing. Too many people convince themselves that it'll take a week at most to downsize *and* pack. Fortunately, since you now know all that's involved, you'll give yourself as much leeway as you can.

> **SMART MOVE TIP:**
>
> Before you do anything else, have a seat. Take a moment to look around your own home. Let your gaze touch the photos and art on the walls, your favorite armchair, those candlesticks that were a birthday gift – all of it.
>
> Keep those images in your mind's eye while you lower your eyelids. Now erase everything from the walls, take away that armchair. Erase decorative items. This barren vision doesn't look or feel much like a home, does it?

Your parents will most likely continue to live in their home until Move Day. This transition is tumultuous enough without pulling their house apart weeks ahead of time. To keep their environment as familiar and visibly intact as possible, you need to be judicious about *what* you pack and *when* you pack it.

HOW TO MOVE YOUR PARENTS

More than two weeks ahead

As you begin sorting and downsizing, determine which of the items to be moved are rarely used. These can easily be packed as soon as they've been sorted:

- Holiday supplies, décor, and dishware
- Rarely used dishware and drinkware, including holiday ware
- Off-season or rarely used sports equipment
- Off-season clothing[30]
- Formal wear

You'll need a staging area or two for these packed boxes. Garages work, as do rooms with little foot traffic, and the corners of larger rooms, too. It's not a good idea to stash them outside because weather is unpredictable, as are raccoons, spiders, and other curious creatures.

7 to 10 days before Move Day

As Move Day draws closer, pull and pack items from:

- Closet shelves and floors
- Garage
- Attic
- Cellar, if you have one
- Outdoor sheds
- Infrequently used cooking and bakeware
- Knick-knacks and other décor, but not so much that shelves and tabletops look completely barren
- Most intricate fragile items (figures with thin, delicate appendages that need extra attention)
- Some hanging art and photos

Also, alert the movers about what you'll want them to pack at least a week before Move Day. Otherwise they may not bring the packing supplies they need in the moving truck.

One week and counting

Time to head to the kitchen, where you'll pack everything in these categories *except* place settings for each person living there, plus one or two more for guests (like you!):

- Dishware / place settings
- Glassware
- Basic utensils

You can also pack all of what follows since they won't be needed prior to Move Day:

- All but essential pots and pans
- Pantry items
- Bakeware (unless someone's baking brownies for Move Day)
- Clothing, shoes, and accessories

The afternoon before Move Day

By the afternoon of the day before the moving trucks arrive, have everything packed in the home except what's needed that night and on Move Day morning:

- All but your parents' daily toiletries and medications
- One plate, bowl, cup, and utensils for each person staying overnight
- Clothes to wear on Move Day
- Anything you're having the movers pack on the morning of Move Day

HOW TO MOVE YOUR PARENTS

There'll still be a few things the morning of, including:

- What's listed above, which can go in a box or suitcase.
- The items listed at the beginning of The Basic Rules of Packing section
    - These items will go in a tote bag or small suitcase that you or your parent keeps with you on Move Day.

Once you've taken care of those things, you're ready to MOVE. You've got this!

> **SMART MOVE TIP:**
>
> If you've hired professional packers (for which your muscles will thank you), you may think you won't have to deal with any packing. Trust me. You'll wind up packing at least a couple of boxes, and it's good to have a grasp of the process so you can make sure those packers you've hired do a good job for you.

---

27 To make it more prominent, use a full-adhesive sticky note, colored painter's tape, or masking tape that's been colored in with a bright marker.

28 In some instances, moving companies provide these for local moves. Be sure to ask about this.

29 This is a great trick I learned from a client. He was decidedly unpleasant, but I forgive him (mostly) because of this great tip.

30 i.e., If it's June and you live in my dear hometown of Buffalo, NY, it's safe to pack the parka, wool sweaters, and snow boots

Packing Supplies Checklist

Be sure to check on the store's return policy in case you have leftovers.

- ☐ Heavy duty packing tape (6-pack)
- ☐ Packing Tape Dispenser Gun (optional; usually comes with one roll of tape)
- ☐ Thick Black Marker
- ☐ Regular Black Marker
- ☐ Painters tape or Full-Adhesive PostIts® / Sticky Notes – at least 3 colors
- ☐ Boxcutter / Utility Knife
- ☐ Trash Bags (the large and thick kind)
- ☐ Newsprint (blank, 30 lb. bundle, look for recycled)
- ☐ Bubble Wrap (small and / or large bubbles)
- ☐ Tissue Paper (for very delicate parts of objects)
- ☐ Large Boxes (4.5 cubic feet)
- ☐ Small Boxes (1.5 CU. FT.)
- ☐ Medium Boxes (3.0 cu. ft.)
- ☐ Wardrobe Boxes (come with one rung per box)
- ☐ Corner Protectors (optional - for large, framed artwork and photos)
- ☐ Mirror Boxes (optional - for large, framed artwork and photos as well as mirrors)
- ☐ Dish Packs and/or Glass Packs (optional)
- ☐ "Fragile" Labels
- ☐ Small Hand Truck or Dolly (optional - for ferrying heavy boxes during your pre-move prep)

Packing List

Room / Destination	Box #	Contents	Origin Room (if different)	Notes
Master Bedroom	MB1	Items - top of nightstand		
	MB2	Bed - King size		
	MB3	Nightstand on right		
	MB4	Nightstand on left		
Living Room	L1	Ceramic vase	Office	Damage - rim

Room / Destination	Box #	Contents	Origin Room (if different)	Notes

Room / Destination	Box #	Contents	Origin Room (if different)	Notes

Room / Destination	Box #	Contents	Origin Room (if different)	Notes

Room / Destination	Box #	Contents	Origin Room (if different)	Notes

Beware the Days Just Before Move Day

Stomach storms and roiling thoughts usually kick in a day or two before Move Day. More often than not, there's a last-minute scramble the day before, and tempers seek any excuse to let fly.

As you make your way through these final days, it's easy to get distracted from one thing, then from another… and so on. But that's like moving onto the next fire when you haven't put out the first one.

To stay mindful of your purpose and movements, try these tips:

- Set an alert on your watch, phone, or kitchen timer to go off every twenty minutes.
- Work on only one task during this time until it's completed. If you finish it, move onto the next one until the timer goes off.
- Stop, if only for a few seconds, and put down what you're doing. If you're on a phone call, tell them you need a moment. You don't need to tell them why.
- Get up and stretch, walk around a little, if it's been an hour since you last sat down.
- Each time the alarm goes off, look around you. Notice what you're doing. Ask yourself:
  - Is what you're doing productive, as in does it

have to be done in order for the move to be a successful one?

- Is this the most important thing you could be doing right now?
- Is your body telling you it's empty or full in the wrong places? (Yes? Then for the sake of your innards, eat, drink, or take a bio break.)

The next thing you do depends on your answers to those three questions above. If the move doesn't require it, stop doing that task and move onto one that *is* necessary and the most important thing you could be doing at that moment.

In the midst of all the final preparations, other adult siblings, or relatives, who haven't been there to assist you with the move, may decide to appear. Family dynamics can go atomic under this much stress, but they don't have to. Or at least *you* don't have to.

Set the example. As dog-tired as you may feel, welcome everyone as they arrive and thank them for being there. Hopefully, each of them acknowledges all the hard work you've done on your parents' behalf.

Should a QFM (Questionable Family Member) slither through the doorway, there's no need to engage with any snark they lob at you. That's all about them, not you. A prime example of a grenade this QFM might toss at you: proclaiming you've done this move all wrong.

You want to scold, yell and/or curse at them. I would, too, because where the [insert favorite curse word] were they while you busted your backside getting the grunt work done?

Before that QFM turns up, it is a reminder that you can only govern your own emotions, no one else's. Internally commend yourself for all the work you've done. Be proud of all you've accomplished! And have a few prepared responses in your verbal stockpile, such as:

- "That's a great idea! Given the amount of [time, stuff, advanced notice, etc.] involved, how do you want to get that done?"

    ○ They have to work? No thanks.

- "I love that! The thing is, everyone who's working on the move tomorrow is expecting what we've set up together. I can give you their phone numbers after you've finished doing [whatever they want to change – i.e., they do the work], so you can call them."

    ○ Again, work. Just don't let them near those phone numbers so they can't harass the moving company or attempt other sabotage.

- (If they persist) "Moving day's tomorrow and everything's prepped. Things are ready to go. Do you really want to stay up all night redoing everything? I won't be able to because I have to meet the moving truck in the morning."

This may come up not from a QFM but from someone who just doesn't know how to sit with their own anxiety, so they direct it at you. Looking for what you did "wrong" is easier than admitting to themselves that mom and dad are getting older. Not that it's fair to you, but you might consider that they may simply feel guilty about not showing up until the last minute.

In these situations, redirecting them, either in conversation or with a task at hand, can work effectively, and keep the peace.

> **SMART MOVE TIP:**
>
> "Dropping the rope." That's the term I use to describe how to free yourself from the spider's web of needless conflict. In the game "Tug of War," two people or two teams pull on opposite ends of a strong rope until one side overpowers the other.
>
> To avoid this same dynamic in a disagreement, stay out of the mud by drawing back from the personal attacks and, instead, focusing on what needs to get done. They can try to continue their onslaught, but they can't drag down into the mud with them because you've "dropped the rope." No more tug of war.
>
> When you drop the rope, they wind up in the mud, not you.

Do's and don'ts for the night before Move Day

You'll need all the brain capacity you can muster on the big day, so I highly recommend that you:

- Eat a healthy dinner.
- Avoid any alcohol. Save that for the next evening, after everything's been unloaded.
- Strrrrretch.
- Dump anything in your brain into your notebook, so loose thoughts aren't screeching through your brain like loud jets at an airport.

- Charge your phone and any other electronics you'll need on Move Day.
- Spend 20 to 30 minutes alone to decompress and (hopefully) settle your mind before going to bed.

Don't forget to set your morning alarm (maybe two!) so you're up an hour before the moving truck's due to arrive and can take time for breakfast. You'll need that fuel because…

Act Three

Move Day (i.e., Holy CRAP Day)

If you've awakened after four hours of sleep with your eyelids stuck open, a tummy full of racing squirrels, and your mind surfing massive waves of uncertainty – congratulations! It's the morning of Move Day, and what you're feeling is completely normal.

Here in Act Three, a lot of fireworks happen because, even after Move Day's behind you, there's still a whole house to empty out. So trot out the coping practices I mentioned earlier (see the *Awareness and the Arc of Moving* chapter). It's likely you'll need them, as well as patience with yourself and those around you.

What to Expect on Move Day

Today will be one of the most significant days of your life - no exaggeration. It will feel chaotic and confusing to *you*, but not to the moving company and move managers (if you've hired them). They do this every day and understand the rhythms and shifting cadences of Move Day. Trust the professionals you've hired (so long as you followed my guidelines in the hiring chapter).

Since today will be especially difficult for your parent, settle them into a room at the back of the house where they can anchor themselves. It should have a door they can close. Better yet, send them on an excursion for the day. It's all to prevent them from watching the dismantling of their home.

Your Early Morning To-Do's

As you brush your teeth and go through your morning ritual, steel yourself for the angst of watching the home's belongings flow out the front door.

Get the toiletries, kitchen items, and any other things you've used overnight packed or prepared for the movers to pack. Collect the following items and add them to your Move Day Bag:

- Medications (if any require refrigeration, store them in a cooler or in a plastic bag with an ice pack or two)
- Wallet
- Keys
- Cell phone
- Important Move Day documents, such as the Floor Plan and moving contract
- Water bottle
- Snacks
- Reading material
- Phone charger
- Anything else you feel is essential

Your parent can carry the Move Day Bag or, if it might be safer, you can bring it. It's best to decide this ahead of time so you don't need to negotiate who'll be in charge of it that morning.

Make taking care of yourself a priority. Move Day can drain you emotionally; don't let it drain you physically as well. You need to reserve some energy for the day *after* Move Day. So remember to take breaks throughout Move Day. Setting alarms for them is a good idea, too. Walk outside and stretch. I guarantee you'll discover that your back and neck muscles have been clenched all morning.

Local Moves - Part 1: Moving Out

When the movers arrive, show them where to park the moving truck. Once they've parked, figure out who's in charge. Let them know you're there to answer any and all questions, then confirm with them that they're aware of which insurance option you've chosen, and that it's indicated in your contract.

Give the moving team a tour of the home so they can begin figuring out how they'll load the truck. Having watched these teams for so many years, I can tell you the proper loading of a moving truck is a skill and a science.

The Move Out Begins

As the movers get to work, observe what's going on, but keep out of the way so long as things are proceeding smoothly. Pay attention to the following things:

- Make sure one of the moving team will be out at the truck at all times. They'll be loading the truck, obviously, but you also want someone there to deter any pilfering, no matter how safe the neighborhood may seem.
- The furniture should go in first so it will be loaded out last. Kitchen, bedroom, and bathroom boxes should be loaded in toward the end, so that they can

be unloaded early. That way, you can begin unpacking quickly.

- Point out the "Open First" box and other boxes to be loaded in last, so they'll come out first.
- Show them how you've labelled the boxes and where to look for which room each box is destined for.

Once the truck appears half-loaded, and you feel comfortable doing so, consider heading over to the new home to make sure everything's ready for when the truck arrives. Have a dependable and detail-oriented family member or friend remain at the house until the movers leave.

Make sure to tell the lead on the moving team you're going to the new home and provide your cell phone number. Ask the person to whom you're passing the baton to call you as soon as the moving truck departs.

Checking in With Your Parents

Whether they're in a back room or out on a day trip, check in with your parents every hour or so. They'll appreciate the updates, including:

- When everything's loaded up and the movers are leaving for their new home.
- When unloading begins at their new home.
- Let them know when it's safe to come to their new stead – usually when most of the furniture is in place and the first boxes have been opened.

Don't be surprised if they're the ones calling or finding *you* for an update.

Local Moves - Part 2: Moving In

When your move is a local one, loading into the new home will usually happen on the same day. When it's out of the area, the move in will be on a different day. Nevertheless, the process is the same.

Ascertain ahead of time whether there are restrictions or regulations about how, when, and/or where the movers can transport everything from the truck to the new home. Is there a certain elevator they should use? Are there parking restrictions on the street? This is particularly important for senior living communities and when dealing with homeowner's associations. (It's never good to rile new neighbors on your first day there.)

When the moving truck pulls in, explain any and all constraints they need to know, and make sure they heed them.

As the move in begins:

- Tape that floor plan to the front door! You'll be so grateful you have it, and so will the movers.
- Point out the floor plan and make sure they know where each room is located.
- As soon as the "Open First" box is set down, open it so everything's handy and accessible.
- Keep your Packing List ready so you can check off each box and piece of furniture as it comes through the door.
- Make the bed once it's in place unless your parents plan to spend that night at a hotel or somewhere else. (The bed linens should be in the "Open First" box.)

- It's easier to make the bed in the new home while the movers are positioning the mattress and box spring, because they can hold up the mattress as you put the bed-skirt in place.

Other things to pay attention to and expect:

- Floor plans are vital, but not perfect. There's always a little tweaking that needs to happen once the pieces of furniture are actually in their intended rooms.

- Movers will usually unpack your items but will not organize them or put things away.

- If the movers are not removing the used packing materials, make sure you know where the dumpster is or have the garbage and recycling bins standing by, depending on where you're moving things into.

Eventually, everything's been moved from the truck into the new place. You've checked off the last box on your Packing List and have made sure everything has made it inside. You may feel a rush of adrenaline at this point because — congratulations! — you got everything from here to there. Use that gust of energy to get some boxes unpacked. (I'll go into unpacking in the next chapter.)

> ### SMART MOVE TIP:
> If you're moving into a community that offers memory support or an area within a community that provides this kind of care, <u>make certain that the doors are not left open by you or the movers</u>. Individuals with dementia may meander out of the building when the doors are propped open and left unattended. This is called "wandering," and it terrifies everyone – the wanderer, their families, and the staff at the community. Wandering leaves older adults with dementia exposed to all sorts of dangers, so secure those doors to keep them safe.

Longer Distance Moves: Keeping Track of the Truck

If this move is to another city, you can follow the same move-in guidelines mentioned above. However, there are a few things you'll need to do between when the moving truck leaves the former home and when it arrives at your parent's new place.

Long-distance moving trucks are very large. Our clients' belongings frequently take up only part of the truck, which is called a "partial load." When traveling a significant distance, these voluminous vehicles need to be completely full, or things may come loose and tumble around inside.

Drivers have to wait until they have a sufficient amount of items from other moving clients to fill up that truck before they'll get on the road. This is standard practice. As a result, they'll make additional stops along the way to load out and move in others, unless your destination is the closest from where they depart.

So this means you won't have an exact arrival date. Instead, the moving company will initially give you a window of time for when your moving truck will arrive. This window is usually from 5 to 10 days, though occasionally it's longer. It depends on the distance and how many other stops they need to make along the way.

Even if your load fills the truck, given the mysteries of traffic patterns, and road construction, you'll probably be given a window, too, though a shorter one.

The window for international moves is larger and varies widely because getting through customs can be so unpredictable.

Whenever your Move Day begins – and ends - don't forget that you and your parents deserve a reward for this great achievement. After the movers drive off, if it's not too late, take yourselves out for a delicious dinner and maybe a drink or two. You've all earned it.

Move Day Checklist

Done	Task/Subtask	Your Notes
	When the movers arrive	
☐	Show movers which boxes are labeled "LAST ON / FIRST OFF" and instruct them to load those boxes onto the truck last so they'll come out first.	
	Local Move: When the moving truck is half full	
☐	If possible, go - or send someone reliable - to the new home (or senior living community) ahead of the movers' to make sure all things are in order for the moving truck's arrival.	

Done	Task/Subtask	Your Notes
☐	Confirm that the elevators are ready.	
☐	Confirm where the movers will park and block that space for them.	
☐	Locate trash and recycling bins.	
☐	Tape a copy of floor plan to wall beside door in order to show movers where furniture will go.	
☐	If it's a senior living community, condo complex, or apartment building: Confirm that parking for truck is open and ready for their arrival.	

Done	Task/Subtask	Your Notes
☐	Update the community or building manager about the movers' approximate arrival time.	
☐	If maintenance staff will hang pictures, mirrors, and/or TVs, confirm that they will be available.	
	Long-Distance Move: When moving truck is nearly full	
☐	Confirm that the correct boxes are going in last.	
☐	Confirm that name of the driver and the contact information for getting updates about the moving truck's arrival at the new home.	

Done	Task/Subtask	Your Notes
	When the moving truck arrives at the new home	
☐	Make sure to get electronics, phones, etc. unpacked early so that new utilities can be connected.	
☐	Unpack bathrooms and kitchen (if there is one) first.	
☐	If we are making the bed, make the bed as soon as the bed is in place so the movers can lift the mattress to make it easier for you.	
☐	Flatten packing paper and remove trash throughout process.	

Done	Task/Subtask	Your Notes
☐	When the time is right, notify the person with your parents (and their pets, if there are any) that it's safe to bring them to their new home	
☐	Once completed make sure all trash is removed.	
	At the end of Move Day	
☐	Thank everyone who helped make it a success!	
	Have a celebratory dinner - if you have the energy.	

Unpacking...and The Day After

There's a reason why you want to have a hearty dinner and a good night's sleep after the moving tracks have left. The day after the move, you're confronted with a mountain of unpacked boxes, and an avalanche of unwrapping and organizing left to do. If you feel a draught of energy at the sight of all those boxes, that's normal. Not fun, but par for the proverbial course.

There's a remedy for this, though, and that's taking a moment to think of all that's behind you: the planning, sorting, downsizing, packing, Move Day, and so much more. On this day after, embrace what you've achieved so far. It's extraordinary.

Let that buoyant thought fill your sails and propel you onward.

Emotions, post-move

A lot of acting out may happen while you're unpacking. You may get frustrated with your parents for bringing too much stuff with them - stuff you had to pack and now unpack.

It's also possible that nothing you do will satisfy them. You try to set up exactly the same arrangement they had in their former home, being careful to place the toiletries exactly how they'd been positioned around the sink in

HOW TO MOVE YOUR PARENTS

their former home. You have a photo! See?

But no! Your mother is sure she had that perfume bottle on the right rather than the left. So you do a lot of moving around and adjusting. Patience easily wears thin for everyone.

On the other hand, your parents may be so glad to be past the stress of packing and moving, or just plain worn out, that they may accept how you organize it. But prepare yourself because they may need you to come back and completely reorganize everything two weeks later, when they're a bit more alert and insisting they can't find anything! And of course, that's "all your fault."

SMART MOVE TIP:

If your parents have lived in their home for 20, 30 or 40 years, they're relinquishing an era of their life, and entering into a new and unknown one. They're confronted with knowing that the end of their life is closer to them than the beginning – and so are you, along with every generation of your family.

You face parents who are likely discombobulated in this new and foreign place, among so many unknown faces. They now need to build a new daily structure, and they may miss the things they'd thought vital (even if they had been stashed, long forgotten, in a dark corner of the attic).

The Basic Rules of Unpacking

Just as there were guidelines for packing, there are equally important guidelines for unpacking. You've taken so much care to get these treasures to their destination in one piece. Now it's vital that you take the same amount of care as you open up each moving box.

Bring a fresh copy of the Packing List with you so you can check off each box as it's unpacked and keep track of all the progress you're making.

> SMART MOVE TIP:
>
> If your move is a local one, don't be surprised if one or both of your parents want to go back and forth to retrieve items they want from their former home, and possibly send some back - and then change their minds all over again. This is part of their adjustment, and of letting go of their former life.

Let's begin:

- Unpack one box at a time.
    - This may seem like a given, but it's easy to get distracted, especially if someone starts asking questions.
- Set the box down in an area with plenty of room for temporarily placing items as you remove them from the box.

HOW TO MOVE YOUR PARENTS

- Use your box cutter to <u>carefully slit the taped **sides** of the box</u>. Slide your finger under one of the open sides of the box and pull it up slightly. Now you can carefully slice open the top center of the box.
  - This is to avoid slicing too deep inside the top center of the box, so you won't cut into, and possibly slash, items packed at the top.
- Pull out each item individually and unwrap it, then set it down in the safe area.
- Take a moment to flatten out the packing paper because:
  - Small items can easily get lost otherwise.
  - Flattening and stacking paper condenses its volume, making it easy to remove from the premises, whereas monster wads of crumpled paper are too unwieldy to recycle or discard efficiently.
- When a box is completely empty, flatten and store it out of the way with other empty boxes.

To keep bookcases, file cabinets, and tall dressers stable as you place items on or in them, unpack and place the first items on the bottom shelf, or in the bottom drawer, to anchor the piece of furniture. (It's the opposite way from how you packed them.)

If you can swing it, have one person unpack while you and your parents organize items as they come out of the box. Make sure things are organized in a way that makes sense to your parents, since they'll be the ones living there day to day, not you.

Put the principles of Act Two's *The C.L.E.A.N.S.E. Concept* chapter into play. It's not unusual for a bit more downsizing to happen as you and your parents find new homes for each item and piece of furniture.

Once you have the furniture situated and framed things unpacked, examine the wall space with a critical eye to decide which framed photos and artwork suit each room and hallway. The items decorating our walls are what make a home *feel* like home. I think that's because these adornments hang at eye level, and anyone entering a room will see them as soon as they walk in.

Give extra consideration to the wall directly across from your parents' bed. Why? Because each morning and each evening we climb out of, and then back into, our beds. What hung there in their former home? Perhaps a favorite family photo or two rested there. Is that what they'd like on that wall?

Something else might be more pleasing to their eye in their new home, or they may want a television there. Whatever hangs on that opposite wall will be the first thing your parents see when they awaken each morning, and the last thing they'll see as they relax into slumber.

Whatever they choose, it should enliven their day.

Just as draping a resplendent scarf over a drab coat can lift our spirits and elevate our attire, so can a deftly placed spray of color or nostalgia on an entryway or bedroom wall.

SMART MOVE TIP:

Recycle! Someone else with a move in their future could put your empty boxes and packing paper to good use. Let your friends and neighbors (new and former) know they're available and/or post a notice on Next Door, BuyNothing, OfferUp, or Craigslist. Make sure your used boxes are still sturdy and that your packing paper, though wrinkled, isn't torn to bits.

Selling Your Possessions: Tame Those Expectations

How much are your items worth? I have very bad news. Just please don't shoot the messenger.

I mentioned in the first chapter that 10,000 Baby Boomers have been turning 65 every day since 2012. Take a moment to calculate how many older adults have been downsizing as they move to senior living communities, or nearer to their adult children. And all those downsized items have glutted the reselling marketplace. A lot of it is furniture.

In the past, younger generations bought used items as they started out their adults lives and lacked the budget for new things. But younger people now just want a table on which to eat and use their laptop. There's no room nor inclination for a formal dining room set.

As painful as all that may be, they're the facts and realities you'll face. At this point, it's not *your* expectations I'm worried about. It's your parents and everyone else in your family.

- So let me arm you with the knowledge you need to not only navigate the resale market but to also be able to convey the reasons why there's no pot o' gold hiding in the sofa or hutch. Here are specifics you can share:

HOW TO MOVE YOUR PARENTS

- The frustration of furniture! Since I began managing moves, trying to sell clients' heavy sofas, bedframes, and their bulky brethren has been a pain in my backside.
  - We have a term in the trade, "black and brown furniture," that refers to wooden, cloth, or leather furniture of those colors. No matter how flawless the condition, even donation may come to naught.
  - When in pristine condition, mid-century modern furniture can fare well, as will rare antique furniture in the same condition.
- No large entertainment centers, as we once called them, will find any takers.
- Pianos present the same problem unless you have a gleaming Steinway or other high-end piano brand to peddle. Donating or giving that upright piano in your living room away to a school or place of worship can take hours of phone calls to various organizations. Even then, keep your fingers crossed. The best way to give a piano a second life is to alert your network of friends and family, and hope that one of them will accept it.

Put yourself inside the mind of the estate sales company, donation organization, or any potential buyer. These are large and weighty items that need to be transported somehow if anyone buys them. If someone does, they'll have to:

- Rent or borrow a sufficiently sized van or truck to transport it.
- Hire assistance or convince a few volunteers to move it out – and then into the buyer's home.

Non-profits with thrift stores have a few other onerous issues when accepting a donation:

- Investing in a truck, its driver, and labor to pick up the furniture and get it into their store.
- That furniture's hefty footprint, taking over floor space that might otherwise go to several items that would sell collectively for much more.

I hope knowing all these factors helps make this reality check more palatable.

MOVING MOMENTS

An adult son once hired us to move his older mother. She had three Ikea-style bedroom sets that that had cost at least $500 per set for in the 1990s. But no estate sales company was interested in her furniture (or her vast teacup collection). At most, we were told, a chest of drawers from one of her sets might go for $15.

This client expected to receive at least the amount she paid for each of her bedroom sets, yet ignored the core tenet of the marketplace: It doesn't matter what you paid for an item when you bought it. Today, it's worth what someone else is willing to pay for it.

Estate Sales & Auction Companies

Now that *that's* over with, what are estate sales and auction companies looking for, besides the Van Gogh in the attic?

Volume and value. Volume, in this case, means the number of items, not the size.

There's a cardinal rule for approaching estate sales and auctions: Don't sell, donate, or throw anything usable out! You never know what they'll consider selling, or what the market currently holds dear.

The first thing any estate sales or auction company wants to see are photos of the items you have to sell. These photos do not need to be professional looking, and you don't need to photograph each item. Photos of groupings in similar categories should suffice. Estate sales companies and auction houses[31] want to get a sense of what you have to offer as easily as possible, so they'll ask you to first see these photos.

If your photos inspire interest, fantastic! Now do your due diligence. Research them online, using my suggestions in the *Hiring Help & How to Do It* chapter. Visit at least one estate sale per company you're considering whether it's onsite or online. Also check photos they've used to market previous sales to make sure they take good photos to inspire buyers to come.

How to Find Reputable Companies

One of my favorite resources for this is EstateSales.net. They list estate sales and auctions that are run by different companies around the country. You can research companies here and find estate sales in your area to peruse.

Other options:

- Search for and vet companies using Yelp and Google.
- Ask your moving company and move managers because they usually know companies they trust and can refer.
- Ask friends and family for recommendations.
- Check out any estate sales you drive by, if you have the time, and ask who's running it.

Just as there are specific questions to ask prospective moving companies, there are certain questions to ask estate sales and auction companies when you interview them:

- How much commission do they take?
    - The average is 30% to 40%, though I've seen it as high as 50%.
    - Their commission may vary depending on how much revenue your sale brings in. The more they make, the lower the commission.
- Is there an upfront fee in addition to their commission?
    - If it's an online sale, this isn't unusual, given the time and effort needed to take photos, write descriptions, upload everything to the website, run the online sale, schedule pickup times, and supervise those pickups.
- How long have they been in business?
- How many sales have they had?
- When can they conduct your sale?

- ○ Certain times of the year – especially May through September, as with moving companies – are very busy, and you may need to wait a month or more before they can schedule your sale.
- ○ Online sales can run longer than a typical onsite estate sale or auction. MaxSold, a company we partner with, generally holds their auctions for seven to fourteen days.

- Do they ask people to check their bags at the door (so they won't tuck any smaller items inside their totes)?
- Is someone in charge of security onsite, just in case?
- Will someone monitor every room as people wander through the home?
- Do they attach a price tag to each item?
- Are they covered by workers compensation and liability insurance? And are they bonded?
- Will they provide references?

A lot of questions, I know, but you won't regret asking them. It's easy to only focus on how much commission they get. But all the other details are just as important, sometimes more so.

It's Selling Time

The items you and your parents' offer for sale will be leaving your family's possession. Prepare yourselves for this by beginning to separate from them in your mind ahead of time. Once you decide to proceed with a sale, avoid going to visit them, because that will just increase the attachment. Your parents' may insist on one final visit. Guide them past the items and do everything you can to prevent them from taking back items they've already committed to selling.

As the sale draws close, set low financial expectations. It's far better to be happily surprised by the total you make rather than the reverse.

Finally, if your sale is onsite at your parents' home, trust me when I say you, your parents, and other close family members <u>do not want to be there</u> during the sale. People going through will pick up a favorite item of yours, grimace at it, and put it down, often with a derogatory comment. They'll also quibble over the $12 price tag on your father's favorite armchair.

Instead, go to a museum, a movie – anything but the sale – unless you want to bear the cudgel of others' judgments.

SMART MOVE TIP:

When you sign a contract with your chosen reselling company, <u>do not remove any items set aside for sale</u>. Many times I've been told stories by estate liquidators about how they showed up to discover that up to two-thirds of the items have gone out the door, taken by, or sold to, relatives and friends. After spending time, effort, and marketing funds on these sales, that company may be facing a loss if that occurs. Please be respectful and have those friends and relatives retrieve anything they want before you sign the contract.

One-Off and Higher End Items

Fortunately, there have never been more outlets for selling your items, thanks to online platforms. You just need to consider which items work for each option available.

The same client who taught me the trick with the "fragile" stickers also had a painting by Chagall displayed in his living room, alongside works by other artists whose pieces draw multi-million-dollar bids.

While few of us own items of such sky-high value, you may have items of sufficient value to consider approaching companies like Bonham's or even Sotheby's that specialize in high-worth artwork and other items.

There are also other companies and individuals renowned for selling valuables from many different categories. You can sell luxury fashion through sites like The RealReal and Poshmark. Similar sites focus on a specific categories or collections. Evaluate these experts and companies in the same fashion as you would other resellers before entrusting them with your treasures.

But still keep expectations under control. I've received inquiries about voluminous collections of comic books, Disney toys, and baseball cards (one collection totaled 15,000). With scant exceptions, items like these need to be exceedingly rare, still in their original, unopened packaging, and in perfect condition in order to be considered.

For one-off, more commonplace items, eBay was the first to bat with online auctions. Other online outlets include OfferUp, Facebook Marketplace, and Craigslist. Unless you're an experienced seller, though, add up how much time it will take you to photograph, write a description, upload both, and answer questions from all interested parties. How much is your time worth and, based on that, is it worth the time it will take?

> ### SMART MOVE TIP:
>
> We had a client with two hoarded homes full of old mining equipment. (All told, it brought in tens of thousands of dollars.) I also once met a man who had a collection of irons, old and new.
>
> I'm never surprised by what someone collects any more.

Consignment Stores

Brick-and-mortar consignment stores offer another opportunity for clothing and, sometimes, furniture. When a pickup is required for something large like a sofa, many stores charge an upfront fee.

Find out how long they keep items on their selling floor. In my experience, it's usually up to 90 days. After that, your items will most likely be donated. If this is the case, make sure they send you the donation receipt so you can use it for your taxes, rather than the store using it for theirs.

Visit the consignment store before providing anything to them. Are the salespeople friendly and alert? Is the arrangement of items in the store appealing to customers? Do you see clothes lying on the floor? Prospective buyers can be careless. Clothing may get roughly handled, diminishing its value. A visit in advance ensures you'll choose a store worthy of your family's items.

A Final Word: Garage Sales

To do or not to do? That's a big question – and it comes down to this: The amount of money you predict you'll make must be substantially greater than the tally of your time and effort. And there is a way to roughly calculate this.

Garage sales can be a good way to both sweep things out of your parents' home and bring in some money – but only if it's worth the time it will take. You're already juggling work, your parents, maybe kids, and so much more.

If you can get your neighbors together for a neighborhood sale, you'll increase your chances of success – and can share the costs and workload with them. As with any endeavor where money and work are involved, consider:

- How many items do you have for the garage sale?
    - Depending on the number, would donation make more sense?
- Who will help you prepare for the sale? Who will help you run it?
- What will you do if it rains? Will it be too hot? Too cold?
- Do you have time to put prices on items?

- If not, what's your plan for negotiating with all the potential buyers?
- You'll need a locked cashbox that includes plenty of change for buyers.
  - Don't underestimate how many people will give you a $20 bill, fresh from the ATM, to pay for a $2.50 item.
- How will you let people know about it?
  - Next Door, Facebook, and other platforms.[32]
  - An email blast to neighbors and nearby friends.
  - Post signs around your neighborhood – but first check local regulations. Any fines will carve out a substantial chunk from your sales total.
  - You can pay for advertising but that, too, will subtract from your earnings, so be judicious.

Open up a spreadsheet on your computer, or get a pen and some paper out, so you can do your calculations:

- List what you'll need to accomplish to make your potential garage sale a success.
  - Use the checklist at the end of this chapter to break down those big tasks into subtasks. You know you can do this!
- Next, calculate the number hours these tasks will take. After project-managing a huge move, you know in your bones how much time you'll need for each task.
- Add up those hours, then multiply them by what you feel your time and efforts are worth. Prize your time highly – don't discount your hard work!

HOW TO MOVE YOUR PARENTS

- Set that number aside while you estimate how much supplies and any ads might cost you. Add that to your time value.
- Your final step is the most challenging: Predict how much money you can realistically make from the sale.
- Subtract your costs (that includes your time) from your estimated revenue.

The number you arrive at is your estimated profit. Only you can decide if it's worth it.

---

31 You may also hear the term "estate liquidators." Just like a liquidation sale at a nearby store, estate liquidators sell off as much of the estate inventory as they can. This term can be interchangeable with estate sales, though the latter term usually indicates a one-time event to sell items.

32 Be careful when posting your home address anywhere. You never know, given sharing options, who may see your post.

Garage Sale Preparation

Done	Task/Subtask	Your Notes
	At least one week ahead of time	
☐	Check local regulations about advertising for garage sales. Some jurisdictions won't let you post signs on stop signs, utility poles, etc.	
☐	If you're allowed to post signs, purchase large, sturdy poster board and markers. Create the signs, and make sure to use very large text and numbers. *(Don't forget to add the dates and times of the sale.)*	

Done	Task/Subtask	Your Notes
☐	Check the nearby street parking signs. Make sure there's plenty of parking available within a few blocks of where the sale will be.	
☐	Determine where you'll set up things, and how many tables and/or garment racks you'll need.	
☐	Enlist a couple of reliable people to be your "security" - to keep a watchful eye so nothing's stolen, especially smaller items. (Have at least three people for this job so they can take turns.)	

Done	Task/Subtask	Your Notes
☐	Determine who will be in charge of handling the payments. Will you have receipts to provide?	
☐	Email your neighbors and nearby friends to let them know you'll be holding a garage sale. Ask them to tell their friends.	
	A few days before	
	Have plenty of $1 and $5 bills, as well as coins, because you'll need to be able to make change. *(It's best to have a lockbox for your cash to keep it safe.)*	

Done	Task/Subtask	Your Notes
☐	Will you accept payment via Venmo, Zelle, or credit card? If so, make sure those systems are set up.	
☐	Organize similar items together.	
☐	Add prices to each item (or collection of items) using a tag or a label that's easy to remove.	
☐	Clean up your garage and/or any area that you'll be using for your sale.	

Done	Task/Subtask	Your Notes
☐	Collect boxes and other containers to hold similar small items.	
☐	Collect bags that you can provide to customers who buy several items.	
	The day before	
☐	If your jurisdiction allows, put up the signs you made using duct tape.	
☐	Assign one table for the "cashier"	

HOW TO MOVE YOUR PARENTS

Done	Task/Subtask	Your Notes
☐	Send out an email reminding your friends and neighbors about your garage sale.	
2 hours before your sale begins		
☐	Start moving things into place for the sale.	
☐	Set up the cashier's table. Make sure someone reliable is there at every moment.	
☐	Make or get plenty of coffee. Have sodas and/or other drinks for yourself and those assisting you.	

Done	Task/Subtask	Your Notes
	As your sale begins	
☐	Take a deep breath and start welcoming people.	
☐	Have water standing by for you. You'll be answering a lot of questions and negotiating quite a bit.	
	As the day ends and your sale draws to a close	
	Gather similar items that didn't sell together, and box or bag them for donation.	

Donations = Giving Gifts to Strangers in Need

There's much better news when it comes to giving away things for free. There are organizations that accept all sorts of items, including furniture. Most non-profits provide lists of what they will and won't accept on their websites. Anything you choose to donate should be in good, usable condition. Broken or cracked dishware or only one of a pair of anything is not suitable for donating.

Torn or stained clothing does not go into a donation bin, but neither does it need to wallow in your trash bin. Some stores and other places accept clothing that's beyond repair so it can be recycled. A quick web search will provide you with the nearest place to do so.[33]

The True Gift is in the Giving

During the sorting and downsizing phase, you surely encountered some reticence about donating one thing or another, either from you or your parent. Do you remember what I said about the World War II generation and those born in the wake of it? How "everything has a value" was imprinted on them? And heirlooms were reverently accepted by younger generations and then, eventually, passed to their own children.

I've found that many older adults equate donating with discarding, as if their items given away go to a landfill rather than fortunate recipients. When a client thinks this way, I remind them of two things:

- They're providing a gift to someone who needs it and might not otherwise be able to afford it.
- Oprah Winfrey taught us that the giver is the happiest one of all – "You get a cat! And you get a car!"

I've sometimes thanked my clients on behalf of these people to help them distance discarding far, far away from the gift and delight of donating.

> ### SMART MOVE TIP:
>
> Because Daisy and her husband came into their married life with very little, Daisy had gone to many garage sales in their early years, seeking plates to build out her collection of dishware. When I met her, she still had dozens of those smaller plates from those long-ago sales, each festooned with a distinct floral design. Although many were cracked or chipped, she clearly felt a kinship with all of them.
>
> I asked her to winnow the number of plates things down to about a dozen. She was sad about that idea, possibly because they represented how far she and her late husband had come, and because of the nostalgia entwined with them. These plates,

> after all, were from their early years together when they lived in full bloom. "I hate the idea of just tossing them away," she remarked, "but I guess I have to."
>
> "Wait a minute," I said. "You're not throwing these away. You're going to donate them and they'll wind up in a thrift store. Then another Daisy will come along and be just like you once were. She won't have a lot of money, but she'll want to take pride in serving food to her husband, all her family, and her friends. She'll love these just the way you have."
>
> Daisy's face brightened as she processed it. She recognized that she was doing exactly what other women from the generations before her had done: be gift givers to one another.

Donation Logistics

After navigating these delicate emotional waters comes handling the necessary logistics. Few organizations send a truck to pick up donated items anymore, unfortunately, though it's understandable, given the expense.

If you are able to schedule a pickup, box, and bag everything before the truck arrives because the drivers won't have time to do so. With breakables, you don't need to pack them as carefully as you packed the items your parents' kept - but do place a piece of paper between glasses and other fragile items if you have it.

These organizations provide pick up windows of time that vary from two hours to an entire day. Whether they're picked up or you drop them off, be sure to get a donation receipt from the organization for tax purposes.

And tip your hat to your parents by thanking them for all they've donated.

What to Do with What Remains

Some items just don't lend themselves to donation. The truck may have left before they were discovered, or they lie in a neglected (and therefore unsorted) cupboard. There's also the furniture left behind.

Want to have fun giving these things away? Throw a Giveaway Party and invite friends and neighbors over! Use tape, a ribbon, or a tag to identify which items are available for people to take. Have the usual party food and drinks for them – and enjoy.

You'll never forget this party where you watched those you care about finding items that will now become part of their lives. You'll be thanked in person for them, and you can tell them tales about their new possessions.

No time or inclination to orchestrate a get-together? Send out an email blast alerting those same people about what's available and that they can schedule a time to pick things up. Or offer your "leftovers" for free on sites like BuyNothing, Next Door, or Facebook Marketplace.

A word of caution

People unknown to you will pick up these things, so you need to maintain your safety. When the item is small enough, arrange to meet at a coffee shop or an easy-to-find public space. If it's furniture or its bulky equivalent and they must come inside your home to acquire it, check their I.D. before letting them in. Also meet them at a time when someone else can be there with you as backup.

Once that last, usable item departs your hands, you're just a few feet from the finish line.

> ### INSIDE SCOOP
>
> At Clear Home Solutions, one of the things I admire to my heart's core about my colleagues is that they seek to find second lives for every bit they can. They've found obscure places to donate the oddest things and to recycle as many items as possible. It's a benefit they give to our clients and to our astounding planet.

The Final Step: Discarding and its Harsh Truth

Things that are broken, unusable, and beyond repair need to go out with the trash. For some, this can sound brutal.

That ancient ashtray with the crack etched through its diameter and a chip off the side was where your mother's grandfather had laid his pipe. The slide projector with the fragmented carousel that once showed treasured vacation moments and made those memories brighten your mind again. These may still have your parents' hearts wrapped around them.

Possessions, treasures, and belongings – though they're comprised of similar molecules, they have no beating hearts nor sense of time as we do. They feel no pain, heartbreak, or joy. The sentiments these damaged things illicit will not dissolve when the garbage truck departs.

The pain your parents suffer once everything is gone may stubbornly linger, and there's a compelling reason for that. *They* often feel tossed away, too. Older adults find themselves castoff by our society, ignored and passed over, treated as worthless despite their wisdom and deep love born from lives awash with experiences. You can help melt away this sorrow by lavishing them with affection and attention.

Clearing Out the Last Remnants

Most people envision a dumpster in their driveway for removing large amounts of trash. But there's also the option of hiring a haul-away truck. Dumpsters are handy because you can collect discards in them over time. They also tend to be larger than a haul-away vehicle and can usually hold more weight than a truck can.

However, they can also become the "neighborhood" dumpster, a place where unlicensed contractors and others deposit *their* garbage, tires, and other hazardous waste in lieu of paying for *their* own receptacle. In this case, not only are you stuck with the disposal cost of *their* garbage, but you'll also have to pay the extra fee incurred for disposing of *their* hazardous waste separately and safely.

They and others looking to be rid of tires and other hazardous waste may add those to your mix, knowing that kind of waste will incur an extra fee from the company providing the dumpster. That's because hazardous waste needs separate and careful disposal, as I mentioned earlier.

With dumpsters, you're charged per load or fractions of a load, and the same goes with haul-away companies. Though their trucks are often smaller than a dumpster, the driver and an assistant put the discards in their truck, a service that's usually included in the price per load. Make sure to ask during your initial interview with the haul-away company.

One more consideration is that someone may do some dumpster diving. They can easily hurt themselves, which means you may have to call for an ambulance and answer questions about how it happened – as well as feel bad about their injury.

After the Discards Depart...

… you're done with clearing the house. *You made it*. Fatigue may flood your muscles. You may whoop with relief and joy. Tears may dribble down your cheeks, from joy, sadness, or a curious mix of both.

Hug your parents, hug a tree, and be sure to hug your pillow for at least ten hours. You need it, you deserve it, and you've more than earned it.

---

33 I've chosen not to list specific places or websites, because I've discovered these policies can shift unexpectedly.

Clear Out Checklist

Done	Task/Subtask		Your Notes
		Things to do and know ahead of time	
☐	Is there a deadline for clearing out the former home? If there is, confirm that date.		
☐	Find out whether the new homeowner wants to keep any extra paint, tiles, flooring, etc.		
☐	Find out whether the new homeowner wants to keep any window treatments (i.e., blinds, valences, curtains, etc.)		

Done	Task/Subtask	Your Notes
☐	Find out whether the new homeowner wants to keep the refrigerator.	
☐	Will there be power and functioning bathrooms to use?	
☐	Are the utilities still working (i.e., electricity and plumbing)? If not, bring plenty of water - and find a place nearby where you can use the bathroom and clean up. Bring a flashlight, too, just in case it's getting dark before you're done.	
☐	Schedule a donation pickup, if needed and if possible.	

Done	Task/Subtask	Your Notes
☐	Schedule Haul Away (may include hazardous waste)	
☐	Purchase more trash bags then you think you need.	
	At the former home	
☐	Set staging areas for items to take away: trash bags, hazardous waste items, items left to donate, and any items that need to be returned, such as a cable box.	
☐	Methodically go through each room, clearing out everything from every drawer, cupboard, closet, attic, outdoor shed, etc.	

Done	Task/Subtask	Your Notes
☐	Place trash bags, etc. in their separate staging areas.	
☐	If the new homeowner wants to keep the refrigerator, empty it completely.	
☐	Don't forget outside - i.e., plants, fountains, sheds, lawn furniture - and attics, cellars, crawl spaces, etc.	
☐	Supervise haul away of all trash and any donation pickup(s).	

Done	Task/Subtask	Your Notes
	When you think you're done	
☐	Go through every room/area of the home - including outside areas - to make sure you've emptied every drawer, cupboard, closet, etc.	
	As you're heading out the door	
☐	Place the items to return in your car.	
☐	Leave garage door openers where they can be found.	
☐	Make sure all windows and doors are closed and locked.	

HOW TO MOVE YOUR PARENTS

Done	Task/Subtask	Your Notes
☐	Turn off all lights and heating/air conditioning prior to leaving.	
☐	Turn off all faucets, hoses, and spigots.	
☐	Make sure all trash has been removed.	
☐	You're done!	

Before You Take a Bow

Just a few things left to tidy up before we go our separate ways. Make sure to check off these tasks:

- Thank all who provided support.
- Return the cable box.
- Ensure all mail is finding its way to the new address.

There may be one large, leftover piece from your project: Have you or someone you trust spoken with your parents about their estate plan and healthcare directive yet?

I was terrified of broaching this topic with my father, yet that conversation is now one of my favorite memories. He actually seemed relieved to talk about it. Life and parents are funny that way.

If you haven't yet, and are able to, pay a short visit to the empty house. It helped me to stand in my barren family home once we'd cleared it. That cliché of the house feeling smaller when it's empty proved true, and my emotions vaulted every which way. But I remain glad to have done it, and I also recommend it to you.

Ahhhhh…

Together, with your mom and/or dad, you did it. You are definitely, and unequivocally, on the other side of the

HOW TO MOVE YOUR PARENTS

parental move mountain. I celebrate your triumph with you!

Thank you for the honor of being your guide and sherpa. You astonish and amaze me.

As your parents settle in, go have a turn around their new neighborhood with them, and cherish one another. Our years here are fleeting. Drink in and serve up love wherever you can.

Afterword: The Emptied Home

A house is merely a skeletal structure once it's devoid of the things that colored in the walls, countertops, and floors, the objects that made it home. The familiar furniture that people intuitively slid onto and into, the chairs and couches that always sat in that corner, or by that window, have now been displaced. No other table or lamp has usurped its position.

Instead, the smallest sound or rustling reverberates in the emptiness, not quite an echo, but sonically and aimlessly careening off one solid thing to another, unsure where it belongs, like a housefly trapped in a closed room.

Beware the emptied family home, especially if you return to it alone. Standing amid its deserted walls, you may find this place that was once your family's home no longer feels familiar. It's a loss; it is final. But the journey to this ending has added to your family's lore, and the next grand story has already begun.

This building, this structure, is a mere edifice, as it was when it first arose. It was the spirit of those who lived and loved one another here that made your home's energy sing in harmony. The things, the adornments are gone, but that glory is not.

Close your eyes, make a wish, and whisper farewell.

Resources

The checklists included in *How to Move Your Parents (and still be on speaking terms)* are also available online! To download them, please go to:

MartyStevensHeebner.com/HowToMoveChecklists

National Association of Senior & Specialty Move Managers (www.NASMM.org)

If you'd like to hire a Senior Move Manager to assist you with your parents' move, just go to www.NASMM.org to find ones in your local area. It's as easy as that!

Alzheimer's Association (www.alz.org)

Dementia comes in many forms, unfortunately. The Alzheimer's Association aids those with any kind of dementia, as well as their families. They offer so much helpful information and support, plus they have many local chapters and resources.

Aging Life Care Association (www.aginglifecare.org)

Aging Life Care Specialists were formally known as Geriatric Care Managers, and they are a saving grace, particularly when adult children live far away from their aging parents. Their goal is to help optimize life for their clients by making sure older adults can live as safely and independently as possible. Their services can include accompanying clients to doctor's appointments and "translating" what the doctor says. They can also keep track of medications, put together a wellness plan and recommend other senior services and professionals to take care of other needs.

AARP (www.AARP.org)

Their goal is to "…empower people to choose how they live as they age." It's not just for your parents! Most of you adult children are at an age where you qualify to join (if you're not already a member), and it has plenty of information to assist both generations—plus there's discounts aplenty!

Enjoyed this book? Leave a review on Amazon!

Acknowledgements

I would not have one iota of the knowledge contained herein were it not for my senior move management colleagues, both at Clear Home Solutions and worldwide. These people and this profession have been unfailingly benevolent to me.

Thank you Jennifer Pickett and Mary Kay Buysse, the tireless co-executive directors of the National Association of Senior & Specialty Move Managers (which is far too many syllables, so we all lovingly call it NASMM). You welcomed me into the fold at the first conference I attended in 2014, and have offered generous support ever since, including through my turn as NASMM's president.

Margit Novack, you are my idol. I want to be you when I grow up. (Read her remarkable book *Squint: Re-Visioning the Second Half of Life*.) You were the gold standard of our profession and, though now retired, remain so. In a time of remote and narcissistic leadership, you have been diametrically opposite that, and I'm deeply grateful for your inspiration and support throughout the years.

MATT!!! – as in Matt Paxton, TV star, best-selling author, industry leader, husband to well-known minimalist Zoe Kim of Raising Simple, father of seven ("That's one more than the Brady Bunch," as he puts it), and all-around good guy. Dear friend and chosen brother/nephew, how you make time to help, advise, and chatter with me I'll never know, but I'm forever thankful that you do.

Andrea Driessen, my insightful editor and instigator, I could not have written this book without you. Your thoughtful guidance, encouragement, and keen-eyed proofreading abilities have been indispensable. Thank you for kindly and gently holding me accountable, as well as for your editing acumen.

My Bliss sisters – Cathleen Alexander, Kathy McCullough, Nancy Noever, Kathy O'Connell, and Sherie Pollack – whose deep friendship and collective knowledge got me through the COVID-19 pandemic and beyond. I adore each of you, and feel warm and snug every time I see your glorious faces. Love you, thank you, love you.

John Heebner and Polly Stevens Heebner, I was so lucky to be your daughter – even if I did have to deal with shredding all those tax returns dating back to 1957. Your intelligence, humor, and resilience live vividly in my memory, and I endeavor to carry all of that with me to whatever extent I can. Thank you for building me a sturdy ship, and for tolerating me as I charted my unpredictable course. I miss all the good in you, and I try to remember some of the things that drove me crazy because, after all, you were my *parents,* and I want to remember you completely.

About the Author

Since 2013, **Marty Stevens-Heebner** has guided families through later life transitions, downsizing, and senior moves with customized moving plans, detailed checklists, and a whole lot of heart.

As a nationally recognized aging expert and certified senior move manager (first in the U.S.!), Marty has—or is:

- Founder & CEO of Clear Home Solutions®, nationally accredited in the move management industry

- Served as the president of the National Association of Senior & Specialty Move Managers (NASMM.org).

- Multiple certifications and specializations in hoarding, downsizing and aging in place.

- Recently launched a new venture, AgeWise Alliance®.

- Host of the podcast *How to Move Your Mom® (and still be on speaking terms afterward)*.

- *Clearly needs more of a social life.*

Once a fashion designer and crafts whiz—which explains the older books in her writing collection—her passion for working with older adults was inspired by her experiences caring for her father, who made it to 90, and her aunt who struggled with dementia.

An avid world traveler, Marty's set foot on every continent—including working in human rights in Chiapas, Mexico in the aftermath of the Zapatista Rebellion.

She's had a lot of lives, but her favorite has been helping her clients navigate the emotional challenges of moving aging parents, managing estates, and clearing decades of belongings. It's the best! (But only when it's someone else's stuff.)

Printed in Dunstable, United Kingdom